T0322139

THE
Crystal
path

—

THE ULTIMATE SEVEN-STEP GUIDE TO
Unlocking Your Power

Georgina Easterbrook

Founder of Athena's Crystals

MICHAEL JOSEPH

This book is dedicated to my family
and friends, you know who you are.
You bring out the magic in every single
day and you bring out the magic in me.

This one's for you.

CONTENTS

INTRODUCTION

Ever since I was a young girl I've been drawn to crystals. Aesthetically they are beautiful, but the deeper, individual meaning behind each of these magic stones is what started my fascination with them. As a child, as much as I enjoyed playing with Barbies and dressing up as a Disney princess, I found just as much joy playing in the dirt with rocks and making 'magic potions' out of mud and worms with my sisters in the garden. My inner child has always felt at one with nature and the power it holds for us as human beings. Even whilst growing up, gemstones were a big part of my life. My dad, who is the biggest inspiration in my life, is a jeweller – and a damn good one at that. When I was little, I was sometimes allowed to accompany him to London where I would sit and watch while he showed customers the jewellery he had made. I was in awe of his creativity, as well as the joy these tiny sparkly stones would bring to those who bought them. I remember thinking to myself how amazing it was that something so beautiful originated from nature. Obviously, these gems were not the type I could afford as a teen, but it did lead me down a path of curiosity about naturally occurring stones from the earth.

However, collecting crystals was more of a hobby for me than a way of living – that was until 2020 when my whole life, along with the rest of the world, got turned upside down. The pandemic not only isolated us from our loved ones, but for many it destroyed careers and forced us to start from scratch – myself included. The store where I worked my minimum wage retail job closed down and I was left, like so many, wondering what now? My redundancy also coincided with a time when I was already in a very dark place mentally. I was suffering with an eating disorder, going through a terrible break-up, was on antidepressants for anxiety and depression and was desperately seeking some kind of purpose in my life. This is when my love for crystals became a source of hope for me and I decided I wanted to learn everything I could about these stones, their properties and how I could benefit from their energy in the situation I was facing. This was when I realized I could use different crystals to help in different aspects of my life and, more importantly, I always had the power within me to create the life I desired – I just needed help accessing it. Between then and now my life is unrecognizable in the best way. I started my own crystal business called Athena's Crystals which has been extremely successful. To be the director of my own six-figure limited company was a goal I once only dreamed of, and now it's my reality! I also now have a TikTok platform (@athenascrystals) with over 1 million followers which I use to educate others on the power of crystals and how they can use them to live their best life, and mentally, I have never felt more content and fulfilled!

I find true fulfilment in watching other women succeed and benefit from the power of crystals. Since starting my business, I have seen first-hand the major impact and positive effects the crystals I've sold have had on those who work with them. I've had the privilege of watching my younger sisters completely transform into beautiful, motivated young women. They have both told me that they feel working with crystals has massively contributed to the transformation in their confidence! As well as family, I've also seen the accelerated growth in my friendships since we have all started implementing crystals in our daily lives. Like crystals, my best friends are all so unique – that is their superpower. Some of my friends are killing it in the corporate scene in London, others are changing the game in fashion while another is training to be a performer/superstar. Whatever it is you want to achieve in life, there is a crystal that can help you along the road to success.

I wanted to write this book for any other young women at a crossroads in life, looking to take back their own power and unlock their unlimited potential through the use of crystals to manifest the life of their dreams. I truly believe we create our own destiny and can have anything we desire in this lifetime, and crystals have proven such a powerful tool for me and so many others. So buckle in, because I will be sharing with you all my top tips and tricks regarding spirituality, mindset, manifestation and most importantly crystals, and how I used them to transform my entire life and unlock my true power! I will guide you through every area of your life, chapter by chapter, and be spilling all the juicy details of how to unlock your own power using crystals. Although this is a book about crystals, it will also be a journey of self-discovery. I hope that after reading it, you will come away with a new-found sense of awareness, you will learn more about yourself than ever before, and you'll feel the motivation to step into the best version of yourself knowing you now possess knowledge and confidence to demand everything you desire from life through the magic of crystals!

THE MAGIC OF CRYSTALS

Crystals are literally unbelievably magical, so let me explain how their power actually works. Before I do that, let's talk about what crystals actually are. Crystals are formed in a chemical process that takes place over billions of years. Crystals are formed in the earth, moulded from volcanic fire and affected by wind and water – meaning that even the smallest crystals hold extremely powerful energy. What actually happens during this process is that certain movements of the earth's crust force molten magma liquid up to the surface, where they then cool down, solidify and crystallize. The individual chemical components and bonds will then determine the colour, size and shape of the crystal.

7

So, how exactly do they work and how can we benefit from their energy? It is a scientific fact that everything is made up of energy, and the human body's energetic system is constantly adapting and changing to the surrounding environment. This is through the very atoms in our cells receiving and responding to the energetic vibration around us. However, crystals are an established batch of molecules and atoms that have bonded through the chemical process I mentioned before that takes BILLIONS of years. Because every crystal has its own unique geometric pattern that's been repeated and repeated over and over again, their energetic frequency is stable. So unlike humans, their energetic frequency doesn't change. What this means is that when we humans start working with crystals, we are the ones who are being influenced by the frequency of energy the crystal emits, we don't influence the crystal. Our very atomic structure is influenced by these magical stones, and every single crystal has a unique energetic blueprint which gives them their own set of individual properties which humans have been benefiting from for many generations.

Crystals have been used for thousands of years in many cultures to bring power, harmony and protection to both people and places. It is believed that every single crystal has its own set of energies/properties that can be used in different aspects of your life. Crystals amplify and transmit our inner psychic power, meaning they can offer insight into other spiritual dimensions and we can utilize their energy to travel beyond the immediate material world with its rigid restraints. If you are new to crystals and you are reading all this scientific jargon and already feeling overwhelmed, don't worry! By the end of the book you will be a crystal expert. Each chapter addresses a different part of your life, and I would definitely suggest not trying to do everything all at once – it can be extremely overwhelming, especially if you're a newbie!

The actual science behind crystals producing energy is called 'piezoelectricity'. In 1880, Jacques and Pierre Curie discovered piezoelectricity when putting certain crystals under great pressure, and discovered that they produced electrical energy. So it is that you have crystals to help power your phone, your TV, your TV remote, your laptop and even your watch. All because of their proven power to produce energy. Crystals are commonly used for divination and can be a great tool during rituals, spell work, tarot readings, or for individuals who are generally trying to connect with their psychic abilities. Crystals have also proved very effective for healing physically, psychically and emotionally, and are commonly used in holistic healing methods and other healing practices.

HOW TO USE CRYSTALS

How you use a crystal can be personal to you, depending on the properties of the crystal itself. You may choose to carry a crystal around with you that attracts wealth because by doing so you are absorbing these powers in your day-to-day life. On the other hand, you may choose to leave a crystal with protective properties in your home or workspace to provide a sense of protection and shield against negative energies in the atmosphere. There are even certain crystals which have very specific uses such as Sodalite (protection during air travel) or Amethyst (which can be placed under your pillow to help with insomnia).

Your experience with crystals should be entirely tailored to you and what you would like to attract into your life. I personally love to use my crystals when journaling my goals as it helps to amplify my manifestations. I do this by cleansing my chosen crystals with incense and then speaking my goals out loud whilst holding the crystals (this is known as setting intentions, which I will get into later in more detail); I then leave them on top of my journal overnight and from the following morning I carry the crystals around with me for the next week. I also find it especially productive to use crystals during meditation, by holding my chosen crystals in my hand and simply letting myself absorb their energies whilst I am in a meditative state.

CLEANSING AND RECHARGING YOUR CRYSTALS

Why should you cleanse and recharge your crystals? Crystals are very hard working! As you work with them, they do naturally become depleted of their energy and absorb negativity from any toxic, draining situations you may come across. People have mixed opinions on how often or even if you should cleanse and charge your crystals, but I think it's a safe bet just to make sure they are all working properly and it does no harm at all. Also it gives room, after clearing any negative energy, to set a new intention with that crystal (if that's what you want to do). For example, if you've achieved or changed your mind on a particular goal and want to set a new intention in your life, cleansing your crystal and then setting a new intention with it will really amplify the energy of the intention and will help that crystal amplify it further. Now, when should you cleanse your crystals?

- When you first receive your new crystal

- Before or after any spell work/divination rituals

- If you've had a particularly emotionally heavy week

- If you've come into contact with a person or situation that's especially emotionally draining

How to Cleanse and Recharge your Crystals

This is just what works best for me and it might not be for you, so when you start out with crystals I'd recommend checking out lots of different books and videos, and doing your own research. I personally like to cleanse my crystals with incense, particularly dragon's blood incense as it is believed to have an element of protection to it, and it smells bloody amazing! First, you just need to light your chosen incense stick, and when you've got the smoke going, run the smoke all the way over and around the crystal and picture a white light coming straight through your heart, out of your chest and cleansing your crystal of any potential negative energy. I tend to do this intuitively, and when I feel like it's done its work and the crystal is fully cleansed I simply put it down. Job done! If you are not used to connecting with your intuition, don't worry, we will be diving right into that topic in chapter four.

'Cleanse your crystal
every time before setting a
new intention to amplify its
energy further!'

Different Methods to Cleanse your Crystals

- **Moon water:** I'll teach you how to make this in chapter three (make sure your crystal is water safe first!).

- **Energy Healing Cleanse:** Whilst in a meditative state, hold your crystals and imagine a bright white light passing through you and your crystals, cleansing them of all negative energy.

- **Sunlight** (beware: some crystals can crack or fade if they are left in the sun for too long, especially pink or purple ones).

- **Running the crystal under water,** washing it in an ocean or a lake (again, make sure your crystal is water safe first).

- **Smoke cleanse with palo santo** (a piece of wood from the Central American palo santo tree, which should be burned for a few seconds until it releases its fragrant smoke).

- **Reiki Cleanse:** Reiki is a Japanese energy healing technique which involves moving and cleansing energy. It takes specific training to become a reiki practitioner so if you are new to this, I would recommend an alternative method.

- **Sound Bowl Cleanse:** Sound bowls, also known as singing bowls, are designed to create a powerful vibration that cleanses energy. You can cleanse crystals this way by simply placing them inside the bowl, but you may need to practise if it is your first time using a sound bowl!

Next, let's talk about recharging your crystals. Each individual crystal has its own specific way of recharging due to its unique properties. However, if you are unsure of how to recharge a certain crystal, I find leaving it outside or on a window ledge under moonlight, especially during a full moon, is VERY effective. In terms of how often you should recharge a crystal, I do this monthly under the full moon. Full moonlight is perfect for both cleansing and recharging your crystals (I cover this in more detail on pages 104–5). This way I never forget and because I've got A LOT of crystals it makes it much easier to charge them all in one go.

HOW TO SET INTENTIONS WITH A CRYSTAL AFTER CLEANSING OR RECHARGING IT

After cleansing and charging my crystal I like to set its intention by holding it with both hands to my chest and speaking out loud to the crystal, letting it know exactly what I want it to attract into my life/protect me from/help me achieve, etc. I do this with my eyes closed and with no distractions (although sometimes I like to play some high-frequency music in the background to raise my vibration and make me feel happy). Whilst speaking my intentions, I visualize what these intentions would feel/look like in my reality so I can really feel all of the sensations of the desires I would like the crystal to help me achieve. To close my intention-setting ritual, I finish by thanking the crystal for the energy it will bring into my life.

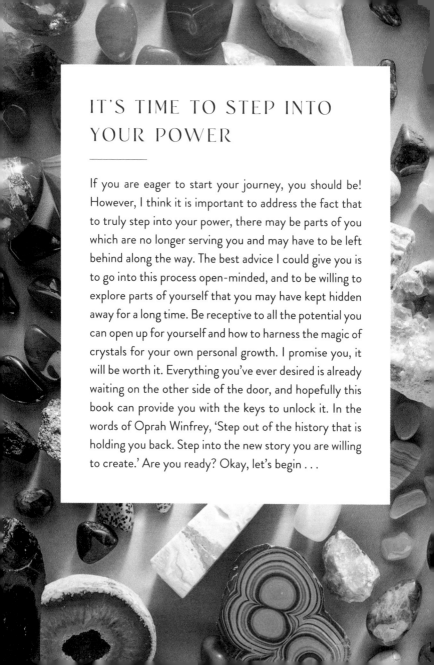

IT'S TIME TO STEP INTO YOUR POWER

If you are eager to start your journey, you should be! However, I think it is important to address the fact that to truly step into your power, there may be parts of you which are no longer serving you and may have to be left behind along the way. The best advice I could give you is to go into this process open-minded, and to be willing to explore parts of yourself that you may have kept hidden away for a long time. Be receptive to all the potential you can open up for yourself and how to harness the magic of crystals for your own personal growth. I promise you, it will be worth it. Everything you've ever desired is already waiting on the other side of the door, and hopefully this book can provide you with the keys to unlock it. In the words of Oprah Winfrey, 'Step out of the history that is holding you back. Step into the new story you are willing to create.' Are you ready? Okay, let's begin . . .

chapter 1.

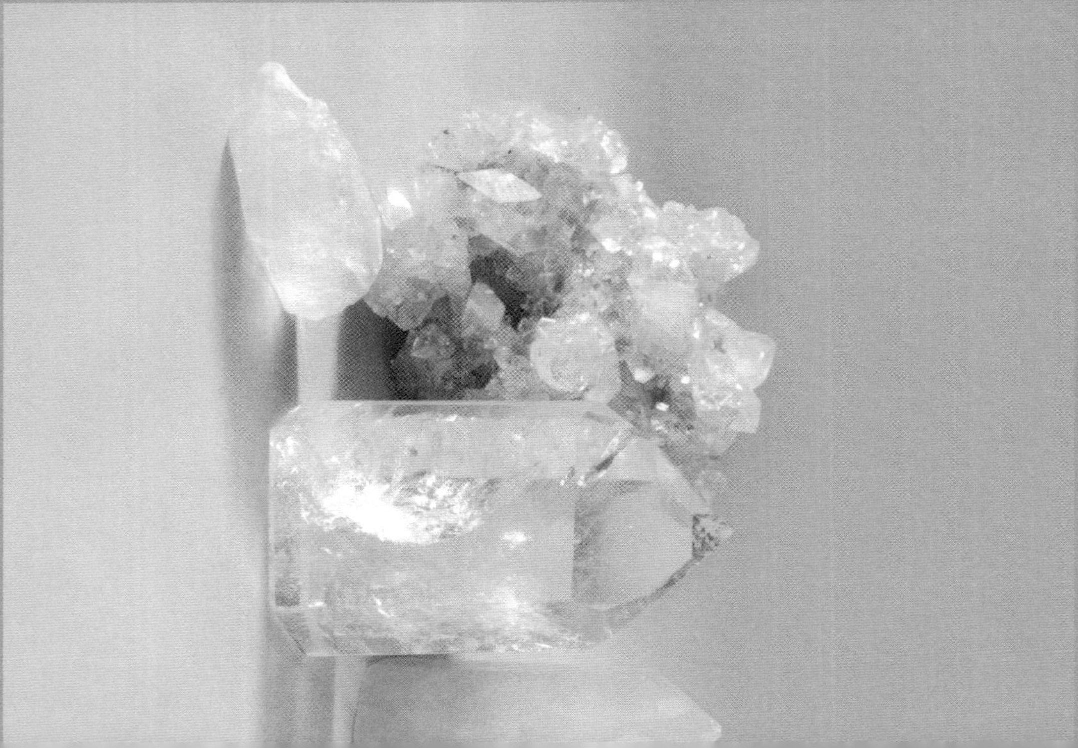

CRYSTALS FOR LOVE & SELF-LOVE

CRYSTALS FOR LOVE
& SELF-LOVE

You may have come across the phrase 'higher self' before and wondered what it means. Basically, our Higher Self is the truest, most authentic version of ourselves. It is our state of consciousness that aligns with unconditional love and spiritual awareness. It is what remains if we strip away all the pressure, artifice and ego. Crystals are an excellent tool for connecting with your highest self and, in turn, allow us to be open to give and receive love to and from ourselves and others. However, the real key to manifesting a loving relationship into our lives is to truly love ourselves first. It may sound clichéd, but it is true. This is because we attract the energy we put out into the universe, known as 'the law of attraction', and so upon fully loving and accepting ourselves we attract people into our existence who fully love and accept us too.

In this chapter I will be sharing my favourite crystals to encourage a loving relationship within yourself, attract love and romance into your life and strengthen connections within your current relationships. I will also share the tools, techniques and knowledge that have been extremely helpful to me on my own self-love journey.

ATTACHMENT STYLES

When I think back on potential romantic connections I've had in the past and the reasons they didn't last, it all comes down to the same thing. One particular pattern of behaviour that I was repeating – and I wasn't even aware that I was doing it! I was looking for someone else to complete me. What this implies is that I wasn't whole on my own, and I now know that couldn't be further from the truth. We are all whole exactly as we are, and a relationship is purely an addition, a luxury if you will – the cherry on top. And only after we have taken a deep dive into getting to know ourselves on a very intimate level and finding out where any feelings of low self-esteem come from, can we expect to have a flourishing relationship. After all, we can only meet others as deeply as we've met ourselves.

One way in which I did this was through learning about my attachment style. Attachment styles are formed during our childhood, while our subconscious mind is still developing, so they are very deeply imprinted. This is because the behaviour of our primary caregivers (normally our parents) plays a huge role in how we perceive relationships. The parent is responsible for comforting and emotionally supporting their child, as well as giving them their first experience of a close relationship. If a child is fully nurtured and has their needs met by their parent, they will then develop a secure attachment to that parent. However, if the child's needs go unmet it is likely to lead to an insecure attachment within that child. Once established, it is a style that plays a massive role in how you relate to other people – particularly in intimate relationships. You may not relate 100 per cent to one particular attachment style, and that's okay. Through self-analysis and learning about the attachment styles, you can identify your own negative patterns of behaviour that may be hindering your adult relationships. So let's have a brief look at the four attachment styles and how they manifest in adults:

Anxious Attachment

Those with this attachment style have often experienced a level of abandonment during their upbringing, or had a parent who was inconsistent with their energy. Because of this, anxiously attached adults often seek constant reassurance from their partner that they won't leave them, as well as constant validation that they are worthy of their love. This can often lead them to attract codependent, unhealthy relationships. Due to the strong fear of abandonment, they value the feeling of safety in a relationship. Therefore, the attention their partner gives them is the way an anxiously attached adult soothes their anxiety rather than searching within.

Avoidant Attachment

This attachment style is effectively the opposite of anxious attachment and is experienced by those individuals whose parents or caregivers were emotionally unavailable or unresponsive to the child's needs. Avoidant adults would normally perceive themselves as extremely independent. But it is not just independence on a physical level, but also on an emotional level. They do not want to depend on anyone to be the source of their happiness. Nor do they want anyone to rely on them. So, more often than not, when an avoidant adult begins to catch feelings they will pull themselves away with little to no explanation. They also tend to suppress their feelings, which can put a huge strain on their mental wellbeing.

Fearful Avoidant Attachment

Adults with this attachment style most likely experienced frightening behaviour of at least one parent or caregiver, ranging from abuse to instability, which is why they now yearn for the closeness of a relationship, yet also fear it. They struggle to regulate their emotions, resulting in pulling away from those whom they get close to out of fear of being hurt. This makes them their own worst enemy when it comes to love.

Secure Attachment

If this is you, I envy you. As you may have guessed, an adult with a secure attachment style can effectively process and express their emotions, thanks to being brought up by parents or caregivers who cared for creating and sustaining emotional stability and a feeling of safety. They often attract relationships that are built on trust and compatibility rather than a repetition of toxic patterns they experienced in childhood. Have I ever met one of these people? No. They are like magical unicorns that thrive in relationships but also thrive alone. But after addressing any negative traits you may embody of the other attachment styles, you can work your way towards becoming a securely attached individual!

I found this sense of awareness was eye-opening for me on my personal journey. With this new-found awareness I could clearly see how certain patterns were attracting all the kinds of people and situations that I didn't want into my life. And better yet, now I could change it. This also gave me an indicator of what properties I should be looking out for in crystals and how this could benefit me based on obstacles I faced due to my attachment style.

For example, I have an anxious attachment style. This style would often present itself in my life as feelings of low self-esteem, strong fear of rejection or abandonment and a tendency to be extremely clingy in relationships. When I got dumped for the very first time when I was fourteen years old I actually thought I might die. I couldn't eat, I couldn't sleep, my heart constantly felt like it was going to jump out of my throat and launch itself at a wall. When he decided to date all of my closest friends at the time . . . that certainly didn't help either. At that point I wished my heart would jump out and launch itself at his head. I was told I felt these emotions so intensely because it was my first heartbreak. And part of that was probably true. Everything feels like the end of the world when you are a teenager. However, this same feeling returned every time I felt rejected. Even in my early twenties, if someone I was dating took an extra hour or two to reply to a text my brain would start spiralling. I would start analyzing everything I had said up until that point. My immediate thought was I must have said or done something wrong and now – they hate me. If they took a whole evening to reply you can pretty much guarantee I would be years deep on their mother's Facebook page looking for clues to their favourite meal so I could get in my car and try and track them down eating any of the same cuisines within a 100-mile radius. I wish I was joking. And if you think I'm being dramatic, those with an anxious attachment style will know – I'm deadly serious. I had a one-month fling with this boy in my early twenties, but he ghosted me and got back with his ex. This brought on a one-month mourning period of getting black-out drunk every day and night and walking past his house to check if he was in. I even left an instant pasta sachet on his doorstep because my vodka-soaked brain thought, *yes, perfect – that will entice him back*. If I'm honest, this was a low point for me. But it did make me realize something. How could I be so upset over this boy? I've had longer flings with the milk in my fridge. Then that's when it hit me: it wasn't him that I really liked – it was simply the validation he gave me. This realization sent me spiralling into a rabbit hole. I needed to know everything I could about the psychology of love and relationships as well as how I could incorporate my love of crystals to assist my journey.

After discovering my attachment style, I then looked for crystals to help with independence, confidence and healing from previous rejection. I found carrying a Carnelian crystal with me had a huge impact on my feelings of self-worth. It helped me to see that I was more than enough simply just being myself and, therefore, it allowed me to be open to giving and receiving love from a place of my highest self. This was fundamental for me in not only my spiritual journey, but also my understanding of what love truly was supposed to look like. Now I am completely confident in what I bring to the table in a relationship. I will not settle for anything less than what I believe I am worthy of. Do I still struggle with my fear of abandonment from time to time? Sure. But I also know that whatever's meant for me will not pass me by and someone who doesn't want to stick around is not someone I would want by my side anyway. I also understand a principle which has changed my life – you can't trust that someone will never hurt, betray or leave you. However, you can trust that if they do – you will be strong enough to handle it.

What is your Attachment Style?

....
....
....
....
....
....
....
....
....
....
....
....
....
....
....
....
....

YOUR LOVE LANGUAGE

Another way in which you can get to know yourself better and really get an insight into your deepest desires is by becoming familiar with your love language. The five love languages are a concept created by Dr Gary Chapman, and they specify the different ways in which we both give and receive love. We are all unique beings. One person's version of an ideal partner could be another's idea of hell. It's very helpful before working with crystals to have a clear idea of your needs when it comes to relationships. This is because the full powers of crystals can only really come into play when you are *crystal* clear about what you want them to help with in your life. It will also provide you with the confidence to go into the dating scene with an idea of what exactly it is you are looking for.

In my personal experience, and based on the experiences of countless others I've spoken to, it's rare that we are actively taught and encouraged to think about our own needs. Which, when you really think about it, is completely bizarre. Love is often portrayed as this image of sacrifice, compromising our own needs for the comfort of someone else. But this is completely false and often leads to unfulfilling and downright unhappy relationships. What is it they say? The three rings of love are the engagement ring, the wedding ring . . . and the suffering. But this whole 'ball and chain' idea of love is only something you are destined for if you abandon your own needs to make someone else happy. And I for one am done with that! Once you have a better understanding of the way in which you express love and want to receive it, you can use certain crystal rituals that work hand in hand with your love language. When I've done this I have had incredible results and it also feels like top-tier self-care.

In my personal experience and also those of many others I've discussed this topic with, there's a very common pattern of individuals providing themselves with the same love language they desire to receive from a partner. For example, my primary love language is 'words of affirmation', and upon discovering this I also realized I struggled massively with negative self-talk. This is what sparked the idea of incorporating the positive energy of crystals with my primary love language – and the results were life-changing. Once I changed my inner dialogue into a more positive and caring voice and amplified these emotions using crystals with powerful self-love properties, my mental wellbeing shifted into a space of complete positivity and self-acceptance. So let's take a look at the five love languages and how you can incorporate them into your crystal practices.

1 Words of Affirmation

If your attachment style is anxious attachment like me you're going to love this one. Yes, we all love to be vocally reassured that someone is into us, and showered with compliments from time to time. But if this is your love language then you will know this is the kind of thing that sets your soul on fire. In the past I used to look to my romantic partners to give me reassurance or tell me that I was doing well or looked nice, but now I've realized that it's a hundred times more powerful if I give myself those words. So if words of affirmation is your primary love language I would recommend that you start complimenting yourself more and, for that added oomph – add some crystals into the mix! Try writing a list of all the things you love about yourself. Don't worry about being vain because that's totally the point. Once you are happy with the list, tell yourself these lovely things whilst looking in the mirror and holding a crystal. The crystal will then get to work at magnetizing the loving energy you put out back to you times ten!

2 Acts of Service

Does the thought of your partner willingly going out of their way to lessen your burdens or surprising you with a delicious breakfast in bed make you weak at the knees? If so, it could be that acts of service is your primary love language. You can show yourself some love this way through the use of crystals at the beginning of every day. Before you start your morning, take some time to make a list of what you need to get done that day. Make a promise to yourself that you will tackle these things and even think about a reward to treat yourself with after completing these tasks. After creating this list, choose the crystal with which you want to work that day and ask for its assistance in helping you achieve that day's goals. Carry this crystal with you throughout the day and feel its supportive energies assisting you!

3 Receiving Gifts

A thoughtful gift is the key to your heart if you speak this love language. This doesn't necessarily mean you're an overly materialistic person. It can be something as simple as your partner surprising you with your favourite snack on their way home from work – it's the thought that counts. For those with this particular love language I'd advise you to treat your crystals as if they are the ultimate gift. Even by simply treating yourself to a beautiful stand to display them on you can elevate your whole crystal experience. Also, opting for some aesthetically pleasing crystal jewellery to work with their energies is something I always find very successful for those with this love language.

4 Quality Time

This love language speaks to those who enjoy nothing more than their partner's undivided attention. No matter how hectic life gets, if you place a lot of importance on date nights and just being truly present with your partner, then this is the one for you and you can greatly benefit from some quality bonding time with your crystals. My personal favourite way to do this is with a crystal bath. Bathing with crystals is a powerful way to fully connect with their energy and, also, to relax. To create your own crystal bath, simply pick the crystals you want to connect with (making sure they are safe to go in water first!) and just add them to your bath. I personally love to add bath salts and essential oils whilst setting the mood with incense, candles and some high-frequency music to really create my own little spiritual spa oasis. If that's not self-care, I don't know what is!

5 Physical Touch

If you are a particularly touchy feely person who adores cuddles, kisses, holding hands, etc., then it is likely that your love language is physical touch. If this is your preferred way of giving and receiving love then I'd strongly advise you to try meditating with your crystals. If you're an experienced meditator then all you need to do to incorporate crystals into your practice is simply hold them. If, however, you are new to all this, don't worry! It's very normal to struggle with meditating at first, but it's a practice worth persevering with and there are plenty of free resources and guided meditations online you can try until you feel more confident. The main goal is simply following the breath and feeling at one with yourself. By holding your chosen crystal during your meditation you will be amplifying the experience by connecting with its energies. The energy of crystals can be a very useful tool in meditation to allow you to connect with your higher self with a lot more ease. There is also significant research supporting an improvement in both the mental and physical wellbeing of those who practise meditation regularly.

What are your three primary Love Languages?

1. ....
   ....
   ....
   ....
   ....

2. ....
   ....
   ....
   ....
   ....

3. ....
   ....
   ....
   ....
   ....

TWIN FLAMES, SOULMATES AND TRAUMA BONDS

Once you feel true confidence within yourself and don't need validation from the security of a relationship that you are enough – your whole aura is different. The aura is the energy field that surrounds our physical body. You know when you meet someone for the first time and their vibe is just off? That's their aura. Our individual auras are massively affected by how we feel towards ourselves. If we view ourselves as kind, loving and beautiful beings then our aura will attract others into our existence that also view us in that way. As I mentioned before, my previous relationships hadn't worked out because I wanted someone to complete me, I didn't view myself as whole. This aura of not being good enough for someone only magnetized people to me who, you guessed it, also didn't see me as good enough. I didn't realize it at the time, but I was incapable of making someone else happy if I wasn't happy within myself.

All the crystals mentioned in this chapter will make your aura and energy magnetic in terms of attracting a soulmate or twin flame. This is a topic I'm asked about above anything else. And if you are wondering what this even means, allow me to explain: a soulmate connection is a deep, loving connection. You and your soulmate will be linked on a soul level and experience a beautiful, extraordinary connection together. Are soulmates always romantic? Not always! They can be friends, family or romantic partners – they are simply those who have been attracted towards us to help us along our soul's path. You are fated to meet and you will feel this soul connection between you!

Unlike twin flames, we get many soulmates in our lifetime. The important difference is you only get one twin flame. This is because the twin-flame concept is that you are two halves of one soul. So naturally, if you meet your twin flame in your lifetime it's a very intense connection from the get go. You mirror each other's behaviours, trigger deep insecurities in one another and play a fundamental part in each other's spiritual journeys. Most can find this connection too overwhelming to bear. However, in rare cases some may find union with their twin flame after all the spiritual and personal growth that's taken place along their journey together.

Twin flames are often confused with trauma bonds, and I think it's very important to establish the difference. A trauma bond is formed from a pattern of abuse that's reinforced through a cycle of punishment and reward. These bonds are extremely emotionally damaging. You become attached to the person due to this pattern of behaviour and that is known as a 'trauma bond'. What I want to stress here is a twin flame connection will never be abusive. I've seen too many times people excuse horrific behaviours in their partners, even abuse, based on their perception that this person is their twin flame. This couldn't be further from the truth. The crystals mentioned in this chapter aim to attract a genuine connection where you are left feeling happy and fulfilled. As well as providing you with the self-love to know the difference between a partner who is right for you and one who is not.

These crystals are also exceptional at healing the Heart Chakra, which is the energy centre in our body that is responsible for compassion and love. If you aren't familiar with the concept of the chakras, don't worry! I will go into detail on all of the chakras and how to work with them in chapter three. You can benefit massively from these crystals by simply carrying them with you, but here are some exercises I'd also recommend to amplify the loving energy of these crystals:

Love Meditations

Place the crystal on your Heart Chakra (located in the middle of your chest) and take some deep breaths and clear your mind. Visualize the energy of the crystal as a green light flowing through your body and healing your Heart Chakra. To be in a true meditative state can take a bit of practice so I'd recommend starting off with a guided meditation until you feel more confident.

Love Affirmations

You can program your crystal with your intention at any time. This helps by focusing the crystal's energy and really letting the crystal know where it can help you in your life. To do this you should hold your crystal in your hand and repeat statements affirming what you want in the present tense. For example you can use affirmations like:

'I am in a loving relationship'
'The love I feel for myself attracts those who love me equally'
'I am aligned with the frequency of love'

Visualization Exercise

The power of pen to paper is seriously underestimated. This technique combined with crystals has never failed me. If you are looking to attract a romantic partner into your life, spend some time writing down exactly the type of person you are looking to attract. BE SPECIFIC. What do they look like? Smell like? What are their values? How do you feel when this person is around you? What are some activities you like to do together? It's important to write this in the present tense, as if you have already attracted this person into your reality – and then the crystals can work their magic of bringing that person to you. After writing, fold the piece of paper towards you and then thank the crystal for bringing this energy into your life. Then sleep with the paper and crystal under your pillow to fully connect with this energy and then continue to carry this crystal with you for the following week.

Self-Love Mirror Exercise

Make it a regular practice in your life to give yourself some self-love every time you walk past the mirror! I found this quite tricky at first, especially being raised in a society that pushes a perception that there is only one standard of beauty. But I realized more and more as I've grown up that this standard just isn't attainable. The vast majority of the time it's not even real! Since this realization, it has become a lot easier to love and appreciate myself for who I am. We are all unique beings and life would be so boring if everyone looked the same. You are beautiful and don't let social media and that little negative voice in your head tell you otherwise! So I challenge you, every time you pass a mirror tell yourself one thing you love about yourself. Whether it's the way your hair looks today, the cute puffiness in your face after crying your eyes out at *The Notebook*, or simply just being you. Acknowledge it, blow yourself a kiss and carry on with your day. I like to keep crystals for self-love above my mirror to amplify the energy and assist me in taking that confidence with me into whatever I have to do that day.

Invite Love into Your Home

Did you know that there is a relationship corner of your bedroom? Placing any of the crystals mentioned in this chapter in that corner will have a wonderful effect of welcoming loving energy into your home environment. Now let me tell you how to find it. Stand in your bedroom with your back to the door, look for the furthest right-hand corner in that room, and bingo. This can be a great area if you want to perform any love or self-love rituals, so make use of this space! *Now you know what to do when you get these crystals, let's talk about my all-time favourite crystals to promote healthy love in your life . . .*

ROSE QUARTZ

◇◇◇◇◇◇◇

This beautiful light-pink stone is commonly known as 'the heart stone', and rightly so! Also known as the Crystal of Unconditional Love, Rose Quartz has associations with Venus (the planet of love), and in Ancient Greek mythology with the Goddess of Love, Aphrodite. It is best known for being used to attract a romantic partner, to bring about a deeper level of commitment, and in love magic rituals. But my favourite part about it is the fact it is great for increasing self-love and self-esteem. It promotes peace and harmony in your life and can help to release any suppressed emotions that may be hindering your ability to give and receive love the way you truly want to. Not only this, it is a highly protective stone; it will be your best friend during all your romantic endeavours and will teach you the true essence of love. To enhance the energy of this stone further and take your relationships to the next level you can make a Rose Quartz water mist to spray in your home. To do this, simply add a piece of Rose Quartz to water in a spray bottle. Spraying this water on your clothing and around your home will amplify feelings of love all around you.

TIP

Place a piece of Rose Quartz on top of, beside or in front of a photograph of yourself to encourage feelings of self-love and acceptance.

AMAZONITE

◇◇◇◇◇◇◇

This calming blueish-green stone is an absolute power house and its powers are not to be underestimated. If you struggle with expressing, or even recognizing your own needs in terms of a relationship, this is for you. I gave one of my best friends an Amazonite necklace last year and it's safe to say her life has taken a few unexpected turns since then. Since wearing the necklace daily she has ended her toxic relationship, is thriving in her job and is confidently back on the dating scene – living her best life! Amazonite is also wonderful at healing trauma, helping you to move on from painful experiences that could be holding you back from being open to love. This stone will encourage you to express yourself without fear and anxiety, allowing you to be open and honest with your partner. Not only this, it is great at restoring balance. This is great if, like me, you have a tendency to bottle things up until you implode into a catastrophic, explosive rage which could have very easily been avoided if you had simply communicated your feelings earlier. This stone will help you approach your relationships from an empathetic and compassionate perspective whilst restoring trust in your own intuition.

TIP

Place a piece of Amazonite in the area of your home that brings you the most joy!

WHITE RAINBOW MOONSTONE

◇◇◇◇◇◇◇

Shimmering like the moon, White Rainbow Moonstone is perfect for those looking to attract a harmonious, balanced, loving relationship into their lives. It amplifies feelings of hope and compassion whilst encouraging creativity. As well as this, it is an amazing stone for stepping into your power and gaining inner confidence. Which is the true key to attracting the partner you desire and deserve. It is particularly useful for those struggling with body image, helping you fall in love with yourself and your body – as you should! It is also often used during love rituals and when making wishes, making it incredibly powerful when manifesting love into your life.

TIP FOR LOVE & SELF-LOVE

White Rainbow Moonstone emits strong vibrations that help you embody and emulate your inner feminine goddess energy. When I want to cultivate some self-love, I put on my favourite music that makes me feel like the most confident, bad b*tch version of myself and dance around my bedroom whilst holding a White Rainbow Moonstone crystal. Definitely give it a go!

VASONITE

◇◇◇◇◇◇◇

This is a rare stone that is very hard to come by and is known in the gemstone world as 'Vesuvianite'. This crystal carries a high vibration and is extremely powerful. It will help draw love into your life by encouraging you to follow your true heart's desire. Vasonite is also well known for encouraging love and companionship in your life with romantic partners, friendships, family and work relationships. Love all across the board! Using this stone will help you move in a new direction spiritually, helping you think from the point of view of your higher self rather than your ego. This will be massively helpful in budding romantic relationships especially if, like me, your pesky ego can sometimes go into self-sabotage mode when things are going a little too smoothly!

TIP FOR LOVE & SELF-LOVE

Hold a piece of Vasonite over your heart and visualize the ideal partner and loving relationship you are trying to attract into your reality. You can do this for as long as you desire!

RED JASPER

◇◇◇◇◇◇

Fiery Red Jasper will be sure to ignite a flame in your love life. This stone increases self-confidence and self-trust, which are fundamental when it comes to being able to trust someone else romantically. It also reminds me of some advice I mentioned earlier, which has always stuck with me: you cannot trust that someone isn't going to betray you, but you can always trust that you will be okay if they do. When we adopt the mindset that we will not settle for anything less than total respect in our future relationships, this is when we attract a true soulmate. Red Jasper is also great at injecting some spice into the bedroom. Whether you are trying to get those fires going again in an existing relationship or wanting to increase sexual vibrancy and passion between you and someone new, Red Jasper will be your best friend. If you find you have a particularly short fuse which could be hindering your ability to form long-lasting connections, Red Jasper is great for balancing emotions (especially for those who may sometimes struggle to think before they act). This will help with positive communication between you and your partner, which is extremely important if you want your relationship to last. The happiest relationships aren't just based on the good times, but also on difficulties you face together.

TIP FOR LOVE & SELF-LOVE

Hold red jasper in your hands during your meditation practice to enhance self-confidence.

SELENITE

◇◇◇◇◇◇◇

Selenite, named after the Greek goddess Selene (Goddess of the Moon) will bring out your divine feminine energy. This soothing, mystical crystal helps create a firm foundation for long-lasting, committed relationships. It does this by allowing you to clearly see through lies and deception whilst gently encouraging positive communication. Selenite is exceptional at cleansing the aura. By removing negativity, it clears room for loving energy to enter your life. Certain energy blockages may be keeping you cut off from your inner divine feminine power. Selenite will get to work at removing these blockages, and once you have tapped into your inner divine you will see yourself as the beautiful being that you are . . . and everyone you meet will too! If you are already in a relationship, this crystal can be very useful if you are having difficulties. This is because Selenite will cleanse the negative energy between you both and work on restoring a harmonious, peaceful energy. This powerful stone will raise you to a higher state of awareness, helping you become the best lover you can be! Keeping Selenite with or around you will also promote honesty in your relationship. We all want to manifest a relationship that is based on trust rather than lies and secrecy.

48

TIP FOR SELF-LOVE

Hold a piece of Selenite over your heart and spend a few minutes trying to clear your mind and focus on all the things you love about yourself. This can be anything! Be grateful for yourself.

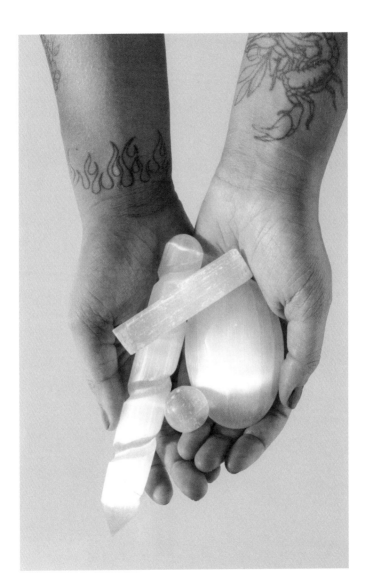

CLEAR QUARTZ

◇◇◇◇◇◇◇

Clear Quartz is my go-to for absolutely everything, and let me tell you why. Most importantly, it is the most powerful energy-amplifying stone to exist on earth. This makes it an exceptional tool for manifesting your desires into your reality. This includes your ideal partner. Simply visualizing your dream relationship whilst holding this stone will immediately start attracting that energy into your life. Clear Quartz allows you to step into your full potential, letting your true inner beauty shine. This is excellent if you are on the dating scene, as you can show up as the true, authentic, best version of yourself. It also encourages a deeper bond in all relationships. It supports the connection between couples, allowing your relationship to be nurtured and grow into a beautiful bond that is unlikely to be broken. The name 'Quartz' comes from the Greek word for ice due to its mesmerizing, shimmering, glacial appearance and, like ice, it keeps you cool and level-headed when needed. So when your other half is getting on your last nerves (which, let's be honest, can happen a lot) this stone is a godsend. It is the perfect little tool to regulate your energy and keep you balanced.

TIP FOR LOVE

If you are looking to attract a romantic partner into your life, Clear Quartz can help you! Simply take a pen and piece of paper and write a letter to the future love of your life. In this letter you can write all of the things about this person that you admire, and show your gratitude.

CARNELIAN

⟡⟡⟡⟡⟡⟡

As I've already said, true love always starts from within yourself. Carnelian is the literal embodiment of that. With the help of this stone, you will know your worth and act accordingly. When aligned with this crystal, your aura will be beaming with seductive, alluring vibrations. Your energy will become magnetic to all those you cross paths with. You will linger on everyone's minds because the self-assured energy you radiate will be that powerful. Carnelian will bring out your brave side, and encourage you to take action towards your goals. Including taking risks in love. If you struggle with putting your heart on the line, this is the stone for you. It will provide you with the confidence to throw yourself into dating and never accept treatment from others that is less than you deserve. This crystal also works very well at protecting you from feelings of jealousy and anger. These feelings are likely to destroy any chance of a positive, loving relationship. Not only this, it is exceptional at injecting a healthy dose of spice into your sex life, whether you are single or wanting to rekindle the passion in an existing relationship. Carnelian activates your Sacral Chakra, which is responsible for the flow of sexual energy. Once your Sacral and Heart Chakra are open you can easily attract healthy and fulfilling connections. You will stop taking a backseat in your love life and start demanding to receive love and passion the way you truly desire it.

RHODONITE

◇◇◇◇◇◇◇◇

I've saved one of the best crystals for last. This gorgeous stone with its unique swirly rose-red, black and brown appearance packs a punch when it comes to manifesting love. It is commonly known for boosting feelings of affection and connection within yourself and the relationships you have with others. Rhodonite allows you to truly be open and embody love. Whilst targeting the Heart Chakra, it also heals all matters of the heart, allowing you to move on from past trauma and heartbreak. It has even been nicknamed the 'Stone of Love' due to its ability to reactivate your heart, which is great if you have hesitations when finding new love due to past experiences. Rhodonite also boosts your self-esteem and helps you recognize your true value. And, as we've discussed, when you are aligned with the vibration of true self-love you then attract the most fulfilling relationships.

TIP FOR LOVE

You can help attract love into your life by wearing a piece of Rhodonite close to your heart. This can be in the form of jewellery or simply placed under your blouse.

---

chapter 2.

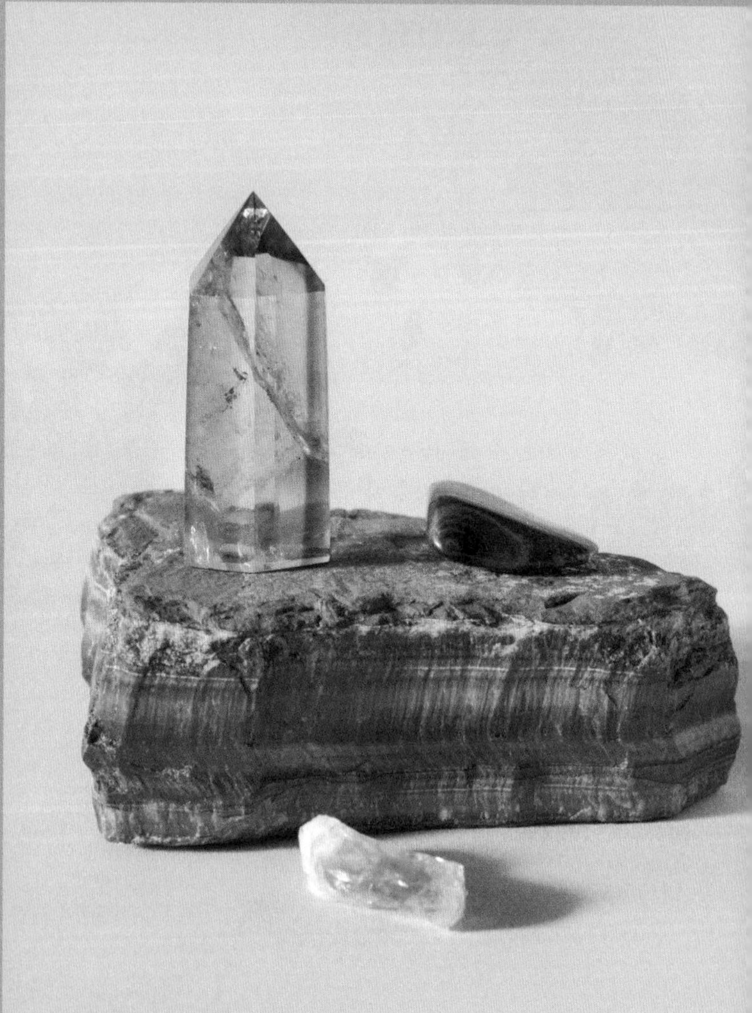

CRYSTALS FOR WEALTH & SUCCESS

CRYSTALS FOR CAREER, WEALTH & SUCCESS

Striving for financial abundance is often labelled as superficial or even evil. Being rich can be associated with greed and many may experience feelings of guilt and perhaps even shame around wanting to be wealthy. These negative connotations surrounding money can be very damaging. I want to make something very clear – whether you are spiritual or not, desiring money does not make you a bad person. Just like everything else we experience in life, money is a form of energy. The way we regulate our own energy will determine what kind of energy we attract in return. The following saying expresses this beautifully: 'Everything is energy and that's all there is to it. Match the frequency of the reality you want and you cannot help but get that reality.' This is because all things made up of matter (aka EVERYTHING) have their own atomic vibration. The atomic structure of humans is constantly changing and adapting to the environment around us. When we align ourselves with the energetic vibration of crystals they have an impact on our very being. Success can look different to everyone. So whether it is for financial gain, social recognition or career progression, there is a crystal that can help you.

Like it or not, money controls the very nature of the human race. Money makes the world go round. But the value we place on certain things and the way we choose to spend our money is what makes us individual. Wanting financial freedom isn't selfish. A big reason to want to be wealthier is so we can direct our focus towards what our heart truly desires rather than living in survival mode. Crystals are an exceptional tool to assist you on your path to success. As I mentioned before, crystals work wonders for attracting certain energies into your reality, including wealth. You just need to be open to receive all the abundance the universe has to offer. It is important to have clear goals in mind when manifesting success in your career and finances. Not only focusing on exactly what you want but also why you want it, what is its value to you? In this chapter we will explore the mental obstacles that may be holding you back from stepping into the most successful version of yourself. Once you've addressed these internal factors, I will share with you my top techniques for allowing money to flow into your life and the best crystals to help you invest in yourself and your financial future.

What does success look like to you?

....

....

....

What are the three biggest career
and financial goals you want to
achieve in the next three years?

....

....

....

Why?

....

....

....

How would achieving these goals
make you feel?

....

....

LIMITING BELIEFS

Limiting beliefs are embedded in our subconscious mind. They are formed during childhood, past traumas, relationships – anything, really, and they are so fundamentally crucial on our manifestation journey. This is because if you have a limiting belief that directly opposes what you are trying to manifest it can make the process incredibly long and difficult. According to science, our subconscious minds are formed by the time we are around eight years old. Now, if you didn't already know, the subconscious controls the majority of our brain. So, for example, if you are trying to manifest a large amount of money or wealth but you've been told your whole life 'money doesn't grow on trees' you may experience many obstacles when trying to have a positive relationship with money. Now, I do understand it's very important for parents to teach their children how grateful they should be for whatever money they have and to encourage them to have a good work ethic. That being said, if you grow up with the idea drilled into you that money is hard to obtain it is highly likely this will become a limiting belief for you as an adult. As a result, even though you are trying to manifest all of this money, there is a little voice in your subconscious telling you that you can't have it. So, if this is you, you need to rewire that part of your brain. This is just one example out of a multitude of limiting beliefs you may have that are blocking you from what you actually desire. So I strongly suggest doing some soul searching within yourself and working out what your most prominent ones are.

When I was growing up I was very fortunate to have parents who had done very well for themselves. There was always food on the table, I went on beautiful holidays, lived in beautiful homes and had access to a great education. I am extremely lucky. However, this in itself created its own set of limiting beliefs that I continued to struggle with as an adult. From a very young age I was keen to start making my own money. I believed that my worth stemmed from earning money and I constantly felt a need to prove myself. I began to reject help from my parents, I rebelled a lot and moved out of my family home and into my friend's house when I was seventeen, all because of my sense of pride and wanting to prove I could make it without anyone else's help. As I grew up this thought process only became stronger. I pushed away anyone who tried to help me and, in turn, became very isolated and depressed.

It was only when I lost my job in 2020 and was at the lowest point I've ever been that things began to change. I felt drawn back to my love of crystals and started learning more and more about the law of attraction. Mentally, I was deeply lost but I trusted that working with the powers of these crystals would help lead me towards my life's purpose. And it did. This path led me to start working with my dad again once or twice a week, purely to scrape enough money together to get by and dig myself out of the massive amount of debt I had gotten myself into. My dad makes jewellery and, whilst watching him and being inspired by the beautiful pieces he made, I had my AHA moment . . . what if I could make these beautiful crystals I had such a passion for into beautiful high-end jewellery pieces? And that was it, Athena's Crystals was born. The point of this story is to highlight just how much my limiting belief was hindering me from stepping into my full potential and the crucial role that crystals played in putting me on my soul's path.

SHIFTING YOUR MINDSET

Once we have addressed our limiting beliefs and where they come from, we can start the process of changing them. We can do this by turning these destructive thoughts into new positive beliefs that align with our manifestations. This is certainly not an overnight process. Limiting beliefs are deeply embedded in our subconscious mind and altering them takes a lot of persistence and repetition, but it can be done. Crystals can also make this process a lot easier. Smoky Quartz is amazing at helping you let go of negative thought patterns. As well as this, any of the crystals mentioned later in this chapter will be wonderful at amplifying positive feelings and allowing you to step into a more positive perspective with ease. So let me take you through a step-by-step guide to how you can transform your limiting beliefs . . .

'Once we have addressed
our limiting beliefs,
we can start the process
of changing them.'

Step One: Acknowledge your Limiting Beliefs

Hopefully, what you've read so far in this chapter has already got the cogs turning and highlighted some limiting beliefs you may be facing. If you are stuck don't worry, this can take a bit of time and I have another trick to help you. Try reading back through the list you made earlier in this chapter of the top three biggest career and financial goals you want to achieve in the next three years. But this time think of the excuses you'd make to yourself as to why these goals may not be achievable for you. BINGO, you've found some limiting beliefs. What did you tell yourself . . . you don't have enough time? It's unrealistic? You don't have the resources to make it happen? The skills? The knowledge? I'm here to tell you these are all lies. The scariest part is, no matter how negative or untrue our limiting beliefs may be, they feel comfortable. This is because they are a part of us, a part of our subconscious, the building blocks of who we are. That's the thing, we write the story, we tell ourselves this narrative and therefore – we attract it into our lives. Remember, you are the author of your own story and you can start a new chapter whenever you choose.

What do you feel are your five
top limiting beliefs surrounding
career, wealth and success?

1. ....
   ....
   ....

2. ....
   ....
   ....

3. ....
   ....
   ....

4. ....
   ....
   ....

5. ....
   ....
   ....

2

Step Two: Change the Narrative

Once you've established some of your limiting beliefs, you'll want to give your brain some positive thoughts to replace the old negative ones. These thoughts are going to be in the form of positive affirmations. These are statements that are easy for the brain to understand, that directly oppose the limiting belief.

For example:

Limiting Belief:	New Positive Belief:
'Money doesn't grow on trees.' →	'There is plenty of financial abundance to go round.'
Limiting Belief:	New Positive Belief:
'I am selfish for wanting money.' →	'Money simply supports the lifestyle I desire.'

3

Step Three: Be Kind to Yourself

After writing the new beliefs you want to adopt going forward, it's time to embed them into your subconscious. Our subconscious mind is most susceptible to new information when we are in that half-awake/half-asleep state. This is because it's similar to being in a state of hypnosis. Try reading these positive affirmations to yourself every day when you wake up or just before you go to sleep. Also, if you notice any negative beliefs popping up in your day-to-day life (which, after reading this chapter, I guarantee you will), start by acknowledging this thought and then make a conscious effort to reach for a new, more positive thought to replace it.

On my personal spiritual journey I spent so much time in my head. Once I became aware of a few limiting beliefs, it was like I was suddenly hyper aware of all of the negative thoughts that were constantly swirling round my mind that I hadn't even been aware of before. It can be extremely overwhelming at first, I won't lie. But remember to cut yourself some slack, you are only human, and negative thoughts and emotions are all part of the fabric that makes us human beings. Don't make the mistake I made of becoming irritated with myself for not being over all of my limiting beliefs overnight. The brain has this funny habit, once you are actively tackling negative thoughts, of replacing them with new negative thoughts. Fun stuff, huh? For me this seemed like pure frustration at myself for even having negative thoughts. Which is ridiculous. So remember to pat yourself on the back for doing the inner work, because it's not for the faint-hearted. Grace yourself with patience, and know with persistence, one day your mind will automatically reach for more positive thoughts.

List your five new positive beliefs surrounding career, wealth and success:

1. ....
   ....
   ....

2. ....
   ....
   ....

3. ....
   ....
   ....

4. ....
   ....
   ....

5. ....
   ....
   ....

EGO AND JEALOUSY

Comparison is the ultimate thief of joy. In this modern age of mindlessly scrolling on social media, it can become difficult to separate reality from fiction. We are constantly presented with glorified little snippets of someone else's life and assume that it is an accurate representation of what their life actually is like 100 per cent of the time. This can very easily lead to us comparing our own lives and BAM, there's the jealousy.

To better understand feelings of jealousy and where they stem from it can be helpful to gather a better understanding of the ego and how it operates. Psychoanalysis defines the ego as 'the part of the psychic apparatus that experiences and reacts to the outside world'. The ego has a bad rep for its conceited and 'more pride than sense' attitude, but it's important to remember the ego is often there to protect us. The ego wants to be heard, respected and, above all, it wants to be right. It is very closely related to our sense of identity and is born out of fear and isolation. This is why when someone differs from our opinion, dependent on the size of our ego, it can feel like a personal attack on who we are as a person. Our higher self recognizes that we all perceive the world differently based on our own unique experiences, but the ego only sees our own perspective as the correct one. The ego thrives on comparison and feeds off of jealousy. A lot of what we experience is a projection of our own ego and insecurities. It can be very helpful to sit with feelings of jealousy when they pop up and try and understand where they come from. More often than not, it will be because you simply want what someone else has but don't believe you can have it. Instead of being honest with ourselves that we simply just want what someone else has, the ego does this thing where it will start negatively talking about this person and diminishing their successes. 'Ugh, she only got that because her parents have so much money,' 'Ew, she is so obsessed with herself,' 'Why is she always posting photos of her boyfriend, that is so cringe.' Sound familiar? Say hello to your ego. The ego would rather tear down somebody else than just admit they have something you don't, whether that's a car, self-confidence or a boyfriend. Why is this? It's because the ego feels that if we don't have that thing, we are inadequate, so the ego then goes on the attack.

The fix for this toxic way of thinking is pretty simple. Start recognizing that someone else's gain does not equate with your lack. Jealousy is an extremely low vibrational energy, but it can be very helpful. It can actually be a strong indicator of what you truly desire. Once you have a clearer idea of your own goals, you can start taking positive action towards obtaining these goals. Also, if you choose to look at this in a positive way, it provides you with evidence that if someone else can achieve this – so can you. In terms of career and success, there is unlimited abundance for everyone. Once working on your inner healing and becoming clear on your goals, you can get specific crystals that are incredible at bringing success and wealth. You can welcome this energy into your life by simply carrying these crystals with you, but here are some exercises I'd also recommend to amplify the boss bitch energy of these crystals:

Make a
Money Bowl

1. Get a bowl of your choice.

2. Cleanse the bowl with incense.

3. Put a few coins into the bowl whilst setting the intention in your mind of more money flowing into your life (the amount of money you use isn't important, the energy is the same!).

4. Place some wealth-attracting crystals into the bowl with the coins.

5. You can place the bowl wherever feels right to you; however, I recommend placing it in the 'wealth' corner of your home. If you are standing with your back to your front door, it's the furthest left-hand corner of the home.

Abundance
Journaling

There are so many things we take for granted on a daily basis. Only when we recognize and become truly grateful for the abundance already present in our lives will we then start attracting more of it. A great way to do this is by creating an abundance journal.

1. Buy a plain notebook (this will be your abundance journal).

2. Every morning date the top of the page with that day's date.

3. Every time you experience abundance, write it down. This can be gifts, experiences, whatever abundance means to you. For example, my abundance journal may look like this:

Monday, 4th July
+3 new orders on my website
+My sister treated me to a coffee
+Free drink at the bar

You will be surprised by all the ways abundance shows up in your life that you may have not acknowledged before.

4. Keep a crystal that promotes abundance with your journal; this will amplify these positive feelings and attract more of them to you.

'I am a magnet
for abundance.'

Affirmations

Programming your crystals is an incredibly powerful way to channel their energy for your benefit. Speaking positive affirmations that affirm your goals and also align with that specific crystal's properties is very easy to do. Simply hold the crystal to your chest and repeat the affirmations out loud and in the present tense. Any of the crystals mentioned at the end of this chapter will work wonderfully with success-related affirmations as they all radiate energy that aligns with the most successful version of yourself. Here are some of my favourite affirmations to amplify the energy of crystals in terms of money and career:

'The universe is constantly providing me with opportunities.'

'Everything I do aligns with the frequency of wealth.'

'I am now stepping into my most successful timeline.'

'Money is a form of energy that I allow to flow into my life.'

These are just personal examples and I'd recommend you use words that are meaningful to you personally. This is because the emotion and intention behind the words you are saying are far more important than the words themselves. Whichever words spark the most positive emotions for you should definitely be incorporated into your affirmations. There are no real rules when it comes to manifesting, and the moment you start trying to give it rules is when you start moving further away from what you are trying to manifest. The main thing to focus on is being in a positive frame of mind when you are speaking your affirmations aloud to your crystals, and everything else will fall into place.

Keeping Crystals in your Workspace

Having crystals around you whilst you work is a great way to amplify their energy. Not only do crystals assist you in working towards your career goals, they can also help counteract the electromagnetic smog radiating from all of our devices. The relentless emission of radiation coming from our laptops, phones and countless other modern-day work devices can really hinder our productivity levels. Not only this, the general energy of a working environment is, ironically, not conducive to thriving work-wise. It is an area we associate with stress, pressure and feelings of burnout. Crystals emit a constant tranquil energy that will cleanse the environment around you of this negativity, providing you with the clarity to perform tasks to the best of your ability. In particular, any red crystals will be a great helping hand to keep at your desk. This is because red is associated with the Root Chakra, which is the energy centre in your body associated with motivation and drive.

CITRINE

◇◇◇◇◇◇

Known as 'the stone of abundance', Citrine is my absolute favourite crystal to promote success in my life. This is because this stone's unique properties include attracting wealth and prosperity into your life whilst amplifying feelings of hope and positivity. As we discussed earlier in this chapter, keeping a positive mindset is the true key to unlocking your full potential. Citrine is also a protective shield against spite and jealousy, which comes in handy if there is potential frostiness between you and any colleagues. The frequency of this stone awakens creativity and imagination, and sustains the process of transforming dreams and wishes into tangible form. It can be quite difficult to find genuine Citrine; it's more common to find heat-treated Citrine. Although heat-treated Citrine does have benefits, I would recommend getting your hands on some genuine Citrine. You can tell if Citrine is heat-treated by its colour: the yellow colours will be more intense at the tips and you will see the white Quartz at the bottom of the crystal. It can even be more orange or red than natural Citrine. Meanwhile, natural Citrine has a more uniform yellow colour throughout and will be transparent. The colour yellow is associated with feelings of positivity, which is apparent in the energy of this crystal. Citrine is also known as 'the merchant's gemstone' because of the success and money it can bring in one's career. It is a fabulous tool for awakening the body's energy, allowing those who connect with its energies to feel at their most powerful and confident. Once you have true confidence in your abilities, there will be nothing in your way to achieving the success you desire.

TIP

Keep a piece of Citrine in your wallet to attract wealth.

RED JASPER

<>><>><>><>

This fiery, brick-red stone helps you tackle problems head on without being aggressive. This is very helpful if your job involves working alongside a team of people, allowing you to get your point across in a way that is respected amongst your colleagues. Since this crystal is associated with the Root Chakra, it also helps you stay motivated and focused. You will be able to passionately complete tasks that contribute to your career development to the best of your ability, even if you're having an off day. If you wake up on the wrong side of the bed and can't think of anything worse than the working day ahead – grab your Red Jasper and your day will flow with ease. As well as helping you keep your focus on the tasks at hand, this stone will encourage you to maintain a positive mindset to handle whatever life throws at you. When my manifestations started coming to fruition and my business started growing to a larger scale, I constantly felt overwhelmed. Even though it was everything I had hoped for, I discovered that the new-found feeling of being constantly busy in order to run a business was extremely stressful. During this time, Red Jasper was my best friend. Keeping this stone on me whilst working reduced my stress levels and encouraged me to take inspired action towards my business goals. More importantly, it reignited the passion I had for my business and reminded me why I started it in the first place. And when you are driven by love for what you do – you can never fail.

This stone increases self-confidence, self-trust, emotional protection, courage, balance, calm and relaxation. It is particularly helpful for those who tend to spread themselves too thinly, which can lead them to burnout. Red Jasper also protects the user from psychic attack or physical threat. This makes it especially useful for those with a hands-on kind of job or if you are just generally clumsy – like myself. It is great for balancing emotions, so it would be the perfect crystal to carry for those with a tendency to be a bit hot-headed or who may sometimes struggle to think before they act – again, myself included.

SUNSTONE

◇◇◇◇◇◇◇

This orangy-white stone with its shimmering flecks of gold is the ultimate feel-good crystal. The Sunstone will bring you a sense of optimism and an inner peace in knowing that everything will turn out well, making it great for individuals who tend to feel anxious about their future. One of the most crucial parts of manifesting success in your career, and just manifesting in general, is the process of release. First, set your intention or goal, then take inspired action towards this goal and finally – release. For those who are unsure about what I mean, allow me to explain. Releasing is the feeling of having complete trust in the universe to deliver what we desire. The more we resist, overthink and obsess over the way in which our goals will become reality – the more we delay the process. Keeping a Sunstone with you or around your home will allow you to keep a positive mindset whilst letting the universe run its course exactly how it's supposed to. Sunstone is an excellent crystal to attract good fortune, prosperity and promotion, making it ideal for those trying to level up in their career. This is because it works very well at pushing you in the direction of great opportunities relating to career advancement and general positive change.

Sunstone has powerful energizing properties, helping you hold your ground and overcome feelings of self-doubt. This is particularly helpful for those who struggle to take leadership in both group settings and within their own lives. Once you can fully advocate for yourself and articulate your worth, attracting the career and wealth

you desire becomes a hell of a lot easier. This stone also encourages creativity, helping you see things from a different perspective and tackle issues in ways you may not have considered before. Sunstone will bring positivity into all areas of your life that are causing you unhappiness; this is a crystal I would recommend to absolutely everyone – it is literal sunshine in a stone.

TIGER'S EYE

◇◇◇◇◇◇◇

This gorgeous golden-brown crystal emits a bold energy. If you are ready to start paving a new path for yourself in terms of success and career then Tiger's Eye is an absolute must! Known as 'the good luck stone', this crystal will support you in every decision you make. When carrying Tiger's Eye you can always expect situations to work in your favour. Every night before I do a launch of a new product on the website for my crystal business, I sleep with a Tiger's Eye crystal under my pillow. This stone is exceptional at attracting happiness and wealth into your life. It also helps to support your general mental wellbeing, health and fulfilment. An excellent crystal to choose if you are planning a new venture. When I was in the planning stages of launching my business I was extremely drawn to this stone and always carried it with me. I found that whilst having it on me I would always think up the best ideas and these ideas would go on to be extremely successful. As the name suggests, Tiger's Eye will unleash your inner roar. The definition of success is different to each person. Tiger's Eye is the stone that can help you discover what success means to you and how you can achieve it.

This crystal doesn't just promote wealth on a physical level; it helps connect you to your spirituality and highest self-energy to put you on the road to your life's purpose. It will ensure that you will live not only a life of abundance and wealth, but also a life of contentment and fulfilment. This stone supports necessary change in all aspects of your life, allowing you to manifest at the highest level. Tiger's Eye

inspires creativity and helps you utilize your talents and abilities to bring about positive change. As well as this, it attracts wealth and provides you with the judgement needed to maintain it. This is very helpful if, like me, you have a tendency to overspend without considering the consequences. Tiger's Eye is also a highly protective stone, traditionally used in travel.

GREEN AVENTURINE

<><><><><>

I have saved one of the absolute best for last. The metaphysical properties of this crystal have been used for hundreds of years. Known as 'the stone of opportunity', Green Aventurine is heavily associated with luck, good fortune and prosperity, making it the perfect stone to assist you in manifesting your dreams and desires! Fun fact – I was wearing my Green Aventurine necklace the day that I was approached by the lovely publisher at Penguin about writing this book! The element associated with this stone is air, which is thought to be the source of inspiration. This mystical bright-green crystal encourages strength, confidence and happiness. The colour green itself is associated with wealth and luck, so naturally this stone attracts abundance like a magnet. It enables you to have a new optimistic outlook on life which will guide you out of your comfort zone and towards new opportunities. Known to be the luckiest of all crystals, it is powerful at attracting wealth and abundance.

If you find you exhibit certain negative traits or destructive behaviours that are hindering your career advancement, Green Aventurine will help you release these habits. This will allow positive growth and change to take place in your life, allowing you to move forward in this new direction with confidence and luck on your side. Green Aventurine will help you achieve all of your career and financial goals by enhancing your intuition and feelings of creativity. This is great if you are lacking a sense of drive or motivation because Green Aventurine works wonders at renewing our sense of passion.

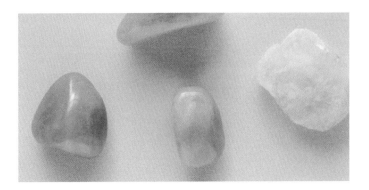

The new optimistic outlook this stone provides will push you to take action towards your goals and seek out new opportunities that are beneficial to both your personal and professional growth. When you allow yourself to break free from your comfort zone, this is the moment real magic begins to happen in terms of success and personal fulfilment. If breaking out of your comfort zone is something you struggle with in particular, this crystal will help calm those nervous feelings in your tummy and replace them with a passionate fire that is raring to get going.

Not only will the energy from this crystal allow you to enjoy your newfound abundant side, it will also rub off on those closest to you. Your friends and family will feel inspired by the positive changes that have taken place in your life and feel a sense of motivation to follow your positive outlook. This chain reaction can only lead to wonderful possibilities, not only on your journey but also on the journeys of all those close to you. Allow this stone to take you on an exciting adventure and help you grow into all of your potential!

CRYSTALS FOR WEALTH & SUCCESS ◆

chapter 3.

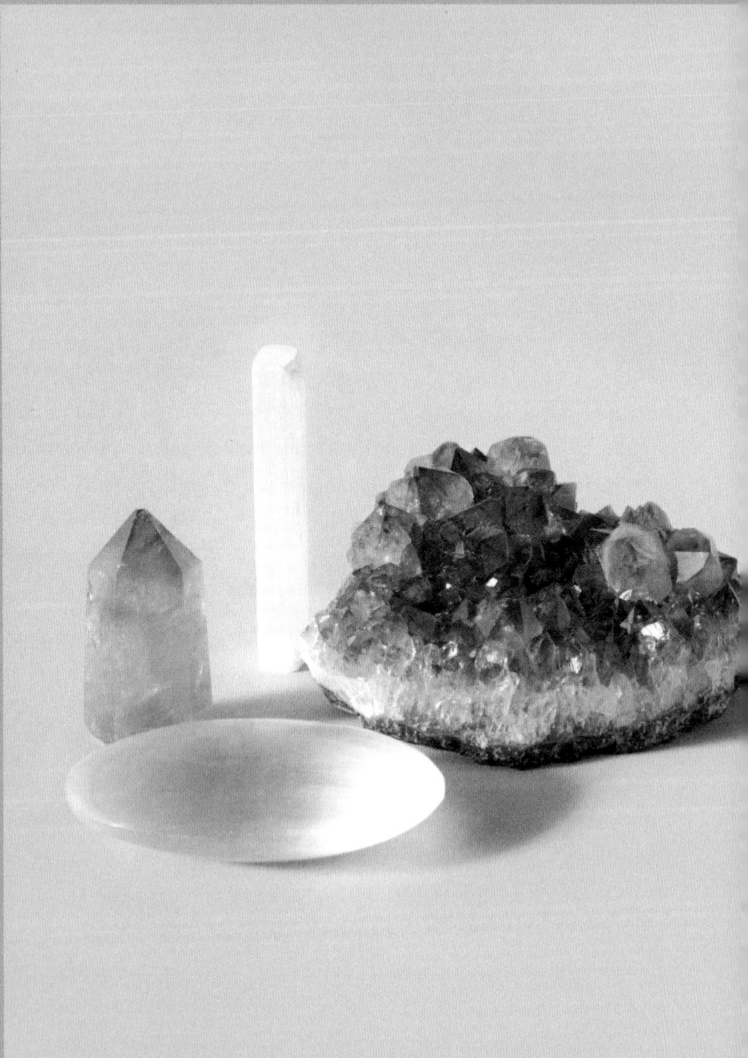

CRYSTALS FOR HEALING

CRYSTALS FOR EMOTIONAL & PHYSICAL HEALING

If we do not address our inner wounds or take care of our physical body we are blocking ourselves from accessing our truest potential. Not only are crystals wonderful tools to help us attract positivity into our lives, but they are also exceptional at promoting balance for both our physical and mental wellbeing. In this chapter we will explore things that might hold you back in your physical and mental health, as well as the most powerful crystals to aid your healing.

INNER CHILD HEALING

This is a topic I touched on in chapter one when discussing limiting beliefs and how what we experience in our childhood affects us in our adult lives – but this only scratches the surface. As I mentioned earlier, our subconscious minds are formed by the time we are around eight years old. This means that what we experience growing up primarily shapes the way we interact and perceive the world around us. If you experienced trauma during your childhood, working with crystals can really benefit you by allowing you to let go of this negative energy that is no longer serving you. Remember, everyone perceives trauma differently. It doesn't have to be some

big dramatic event that mirrors an episode of *EastEnders* – it can simply be a painful experience that still triggers you in your adult life. Behind every angry outburst or seemingly unsolicited behaviour there is a wounded inner child within you looking to be reassured.

I'm going to share a personal story with you now to give you an example of how powerful having an unhealed inner child can be. I have always had a very up-and-down relationship with food. Whenever I hit a rough patch in my life my go-to would be to either over-eat or stop eating altogether. I hit my lowest point mentally when I was eighteen years old and, as a result, developed an eating disorder. The only way I could think to take the pain away from what I was feeling in my mind was to limit the calories I was putting into my body. It gave me a sense of control but also a sense of accomplishment when I'd see the weight dropping off every time I stepped on the scales.

However, this cycle continued until I was very unwell indeed. I was taking multiple vitamins to provide my body with what it needed in order to function, but I was extremely underweight, and at high risk of developing anaemia and becoming infertile. There are so many things I want to experience in life and after hearing all of this information from the doctors I realized something needed to change. I decided I wanted to get better but knew this wasn't going to be a simple fix, and that I needed to completely change my mindset.

This was when I really got into learning about inner child healing, crystals, manifestation and the power of the mind. I bought myself an Amethyst crystal (known as the all-healer) and started journaling.

I knew if I wanted to get better I had to get to the root of what was making me feel this way. Whilst wearing my Amethyst crystal I wrote pages and pages exploring these feelings and where they may have come from. Before journaling I had originally put it down to the superficial stuff – wanting to be skinny, look more desirable, etc., etc., but this was false.

When I started writing about my childhood I realized something: I always felt like I was fighting for attention as a child. Now, don't get me wrong, I have wonderful parents who absolutely adore me and couldn't have done more for me growing up. This being said, I was the oldest of four siblings (five now!), and with a household full of strong personalities – as you can imagine, it was hard to get a word in edgeways. I always knew that if I wanted to get my parents' full attention there was one sure way that would work – to pretend to be unwell. You know how it is – you're young, you stumble into your parents' bedroom giving a very convincing performance of being bent over in agony from excruciating stomach pains. Before you know it, your Oscar-winning performance has landed you a day off school, lots of cuddles and at least one of your parents waiting on you hand and foot all day long. As I continued to journal, I came to the realization that my eating disorder wasn't to do with body image at all. Whenever I felt a lack of attention, whether it be a rocky patch in a relationship, not feeling successful in my career or even arguing with friends, my reflex reaction was to stop eating. This is because I was repeating a behaviour that was deeply embedded in my subconscious as a child. And this behaviour was a simple belief – I will be treated the way I desire if I make myself ill. Now, of course, as an adult I know this is completely untrue. But once I finally got to the root of what was causing me to have this negative relationship with eating and, therefore, my health, I was able to tackle this problem from a completely new perspective.

It's important not to blame your inner child for the issues it may be causing now. Our brains have a funny way of perceiving the world around us (especially whilst we are still developing) and creating safety measures for ourselves that we aren't always even aware of. Only when we learn to accept ourselves fully, the good, bad and the ugly, can we step into our truest potential. And if you're not sure where to start, I would recommend showing your inner child some love. Here are my favourite ways to get in touch with your inner child:

◇ Try to acknowledge and journal any needs you felt were unmet as you were growing up.

◇ Write a letter to your inner child validating their experiences and how you plan to re-parent yourself.

◇ Engage in playful activities such as eating your favourite sweet treats, being silly/playful and laughing with your friends.

◇ Reassure yourself every day that you are there for yourself and treat yourself with kindness and compassion always.

Do you feel like all of your needs were met growing up? Explain.

....
....
....
....
....
....
....

How are you able to provide yourself with these unmet needs now?

....
....
....
....
....
....
....

SHADOW WORK

Another crucial part of my healing journey was accessing my shadow self through shadow work. Your shadow self is basically the part of you that you don't like very much. The part that you try and keep hidden away. But shadow work is about understanding that part of us and why we don't like it. And then through learning more deeply about ourselves, we can use this knowledge to feel more empowered and accepted within ourselves. The 'shadow self' is a term invented by psychoanalyst Carl Jung. Shadow work is simply shining a light on our shadow self to see those wounded inner-child parts that are wanting to be processed and healed.

You can find lots of shadow work books or prompts online to help you start, but let me tell you about my personal, preferred way to do it . . .

Whenever I experience a feeling I don't like, whether that be jealousy, sadness, loneliness, etc., I get out my journal. I then try to lean into that feeling and express my thoughts on the paper. I really just explore how my mind is processing information around me in that present moment, writing whatever comes to mind and why I believe it is making me feel that way. I keep writing and writing, going deeper and deeper until I figure out where the root of that emotion has come from. And sometimes this has shocked me. There have been times I have written for pages and pages and gone way back to my young childhood years, like I did with my eating disorder. The benefit of this is you can then understand how that triggers you in other areas of your life. You will have a lot more control over those feelings when you understand where they come from and, therefore, they then have less power over you. This helps you see that you are not defined by your emotions, you are just a normal human being experiencing a particular emotion. How you then perceive and process emotion is different for each individual dependent on their own unique life experiences. Now, shadow work can be really heavy so grab yourself a nice cup of tea while you're writing – and have a friend on speed dial to call for a cry if needed!

Crystals have really assisted me in my shadow work practice. When writing in this particular way I always keep my Smoky Quartz sphere on my lap. This is because Smoky Quartz is a protective crystal that helps draw out negative energy and assists you in moving on from painful experiences. Also, when a crystal comes in the shape of a sphere it means it is particularly great for relieving stress and encourages us to feel whole, fulfilled and content.

MEDITATION

Over the past two decades, more and more scientists have studied the benefits of mindfulness practices on our physical and mental wellbeing. Regular meditation has been scientifically proven to improve attention span, reduce stress and improve our mental and physical health – particularly depression, chronic pain and anxiety. You can enhance your meditation experience through adding certain crystals to your practice. Incorporating crystals into your meditation ritual can help you achieve a specific outcome or just generally deepen your practice. This is because crystals are known to align you with your intuition, allowing you to raise your consciousness and awareness and, therefore, tap into your highest self with a lot more ease.

If you're just starting your spiritual journey and want to get into meditation but you are finding it all slightly overwhelming, I would recommend starting with 'walking meditation'. This is a form of meditation practice I would do at the beginning of my spiritual and healing journey that I wasn't even aware of, but it helped me so much! Now, everyone views and defines meditation differently. But I believe at its very core, it is simply about being present and being in the moment. We spend so much of our lives on our phones, or worrying about the future, or overthinking the past. It's very rare that we find time to just sit and be present with ourselves in the moment with no thoughts running round and round in our heads demanding our attention. Walking meditation is basically going out on a walk but making a conscious effort to keep yourself grounded in the present moment. Leave your phone at home! Focus on your breathing. Look at the colour of the sky. Notice the colours of the flowers. Notice the smells in the air, how the ground feels under your feet. Just get in touch with nature and live in that moment! That, to me, was massive to my spiritual journey and had a major positive impact on my mental wellbeing. I would also recommend placing any of the crystals mentioned later in this chapter in your pocket to amplify the benefits of this practice.

CHAKRAS

Our chakras are the energy centres of our body – our inner universe. Your chakras help regulate your mood and physical health. There are seven chakras in total and they are all responsible for different parts of your physical and spiritual being. Past pain or trauma can leave your chakras misaligned or even blocked, which greatly affects the overall functioning of your energy and aura. When our chakras are unbalanced, it can make us feel stuck or thrown off in certain areas of our life. If you are looking for help with a particular chakra, crystals are the perfect way to go. Every single crystal is associated with a particular chakra. An easy way to differentiate and identify which crystal can help with a particular chakra is through their colour. Each chakra is associated with a different colour so, generally speaking, you can use a crystal that corresponds colour-wise to that chakra to bring it back into alignment. There is no limit to how many crystals you can use at one time. If you are a beginner I would recommend starting out working with one crystal and one chakra. As you become more confident, let your intuition guide you on how many crystals you would like to work with. If you haven't heard the term intuition before, don't worry! I will go into detail on how to connect and trust your intuition in chapter four. But for now, let's break down each chakra and the crystals that correspond to them.

Root Chakra

Your Root Chakra is located at the base of your spine. This energy centre is responsible for our connection with the earth and for grounding us. This chakra also contributes to our general feelings of security and having our basic emotional, physical and financial needs met. The colour associated with this chakra is red, so if your Root Chakra needs some TLC then get yourself some red crystals. These crystals' colour is, generally speaking, also helpful in assisting us with our energy and motivation levels. Working with red crystals will help bring you back into alignment and encourage you to take inspired action towards your goals.

Sacral Chakra

The Sacral Chakra is located just beneath your belly button. It is responsible for how we feel and process our emotions. It is also associated with our intimate relationships with ourselves and others including factors such as sexuality, sensuality and pleasure. When this chakra is blocked you will also notice a negative impact on your creativity levels. Using orange crystals can help bring the Sacral Chakra back into alignment and restore the energy of your feminine flow.

Solar Plexus Chakra

Confidence is an energy we can tap into whenever we choose. The Solar Plexus Chakra is located just beneath the ribcage and gives us the ability to sense our personal power. It also plays a part in determining our identity and beliefs. When this chakra is misaligned, our personal power is difficult to obtain and maintain and you may feel a lack of motivation and drive. You can help heal blockages in this chakra with yellow crystals.

Heart Chakra

This chakra can be found in the centre of the chest and, as you might have guessed, is responsible for all things love and self-love. In addition, this chakra is associated with forgiveness, compassion and acceptance. Having blockages in the Heart Chakra will greatly impact the connections you are able to form with yourself, others and the world around you. Our highest self is aligned with the vibration of unconditional love, so it is important that we take good care of our Heart Chakra. Both pink and green crystals can be used to give this chakra a bit of love and attention if needed.

Throat Chakra

The Throat Chakra covers all general forms of communication. Struggling to speak your truth could be an indicator that your Throat Chakra is blocked. It is important to take care of this chakra so that you can effectively address and communicate your needs and desires to those around you. The colour associated with the Throat Chakra is blue – mostly light shades of it – so using crystals of that colour can help you with any blockages you have in this chakra.

Third Eye Chakra

Located on your forehead, just above the middle of the brows, is the Third Eye Chakra – also commonly referred to as the pineal gland. This chakra is responsible for your intuition and will play a crucial role in your spiritual journey. It relates to your sense of spiritual awareness and allows you to visualize beyond the physical dimension of what the eyes can see. When your Third Eye Chakra is open, you will have a greater connection with your inner wisdom and knowing. You can use blue-shaded, mostly indigo or light-purple, crystals to help aid this chakra.

Crown Chakra

This chakra is the one that goes beyond what we feel and know about ourselves. Found in the crown of the head, it is associated with our connection to a higher power, source and the universe. It relates to a state of pure consciousness and being a part of something greater than ourselves. The colour associated with this chakra is violet/dark purple and so crystals of this colour are commonly used to heal blockages in the Crown Chakra.

Chakra Balancing Exercise

Laying crystals that directly correspond to each chakra on the body will work wonders at bringing your chakras back into alignment. You can focus on one chakra at a time or lie back and do them all at once. Simply place the colour crystal that matches the energy centre on that chakra whilst meditating. You can set the intention with the crystal before you begin to heal that particular chakra: you can say this intention out loud to the crystal or in your head, whatever feels right for you. The crystals will then get to work on activating and rebalancing these areas. There are also lots of guided chakra healing meditations online if you don't know where to start! I personally love the 'Chakra Meditation Cleansing, Balancing and Healing with Guided Hypnosis Activation' by Micheal Sealey on YouTube and the '10-Minute Chakra Balance Guided Meditation for Positive Energy' by Great Meditation which you can also find on YouTube.

FULL MOON MAGIC

Full moons hold an extremely powerful energy and it is my favourite time to charge my crystals. Now, let's talk about why you should cleanse and charge your crystals. Crystals are very hard working and as you work with them they do naturally become depleted of energy and absorb negativity from both toxic/draining people and situations you may come into contact with. Although some people have mixed opinions on how important it is, and on how often you should cleanse your crystals, I believe it is a good way of ensuring that any negativity that may have penetrated your aura is dissipated. Each crystal has its own method of charging that is unique to its individual properties. However, if you are unsure I find leaving them under the light of a full moon to be very effective for both cleansing and charging. This has become a staple practice for me every full moon. To do this I simply leave my crystals outside or on a window ledge, under the moonlight, and retrieve them the following morning. Not only is it my favourite time to charge and cleanse my crystals, but it is also known for being the most powerful time to release any negative energy that is no longer serving us. This is because the full moon is associated with the completion of a cycle. Working with crystals and setting intentions of what energy I would like to release every full moon has completely changed my life. So allow me to share my favourite ritual with you . . .

Full Moon
Release Ritual

Write a list of any situations, people, destructive behaviours or thought patterns you would like to release in statements starting 'I release . . .' For example: 'I release the need to be validated by others.'

◇ After writing this list, have a literal cleanse. Have a bath or a shower and visualize yourself cleansing this negative energy off of you.

◇ You can then dispose of this list by burning, burying or simply ripping it up.

◇ After destroying your list, grab a fresh sheet of paper and write down the following affirmation: 'I now let go of all that is not in alignment with my highest purpose and open myself to receive all that I desire.'

◇ Fold the piece of paper with the affirmation written on it towards you to really draw in that energy.

◇ Take the folded paper outside, under the full moon, and place it under a container of moon water (see below).

Then you can place your crystals on top of the container of moon water – you can choose crystals you are simply intuitively drawn to or ones that specifically contain properties that align with the energy you are trying to draw into your life.

Leave the crystals, moon water and paper outside under the full moon and retrieve the following morning. This will allow the crystals and the moon water to be charged with the positive intention, ready to welcome in new blessings!

How to Make Moon Water

1. Take any jar or container (as long as it has a lid).

2. Cleanse the container inside and out (I like to use incense, but you can also use Palo Santo, Sage, Sound or Energy Cleansing).

3. Whilst cleansing the container, visualize positive intentions.

4. Fill the container with water and place outside or on a window ledge to absorb the full moon's energy overnight.

5. You can place written manifestations underneath and crystals on top to amplify the energy (this charges the water and crystals with your positive intentions).

Different Ways to Use Moon Water

◇ Drink it! I especially like adding it to herbal teas.

◇ Use it in cooking.

◇ Add some moon water to your cleaning solutions to give your home an energetic cleansing.

◇ Pop some in an empty spray bottle with some essential oils to use on clothing or to spray around your home.

◇ Water plants with it.

◇ For cleansing crystals (make sure they are water safe first!).

◇ Add to your bath for a literal spiritual oasis pamper session!

Now I've established all my favourite healing tips and tricks, let's get into my favourite crystals to assist you on your healing journey!

AMETHYST

◇◇◇◇◇◇◇

We are starting off strong with Amethyst. It's known as The 'All-Healer', due to being one of the most effective stones for healing work on earth. This crystal is also known for being particularly useful for helping those who struggle with addiction. It is amazing for anyone who is feeling exhausted or stressed due to its calming nature. Amethyst is my absolute go-to when I'm feeling overwhelmed and in need of some TLC. It also relieves feelings of sadness and grief, making it wonderful for those who are just starting out their healing journey. As well as this, it encourages individuals to give themselves the love they need to allow their energy to flow again. This helps prevent burnout and enables you to continue to show up for yourself and those around you as the happiest, healthiest version of yourself. Because Amethyst is associated with the Third Eye Chakra it helps to open your intuition and enhance your psychic abilities whilst protecting you against psychic attacks. This magical-looking purple crystal is pretty famous for soothing headaches and, in my personal experience, helping with hangovers! I would recommend Amethyst as a must-have for any beginner because it works so well at releasing negative thoughts from the mind. And who wouldn't want that? Here is an easy exercise you can do with Amethyst to help relieve the mind of negativity:

Lie down and place a piece of Amethyst on your Third Eye Chakra and visualize the crystal drawing out all the negative thoughts and taking them away up into the atmosphere.

TIP FOR HEALING

*If you struggle with insomnia or nightmares, sleep with a piece of
Amethyst under your pillow to ensure a peaceful night's sleep!*

SODALITE

◇◇◇◇◇◇◇◇

Known as 'the stone of logic', this rich royal-blue crystal mottled with white veins emits a tranquil energy that clears the mind and provokes deep thought. This is wonderful if you tend to be overly emotional as it gives you the ability to see things from a more logical and rational perspective. This is the ultimate calming crystal and is ideal for those who suffer with anxiety and panic attacks, or are oversensitive, defensive or impulsive. Sodalite also opens up spiritual perception and encourages trust and companionship in your life. This is because it allows you to trust your intuition and encourages you to communicate your feelings. Sodalite is associated with the Third Eye and Throat Chakras, making it very useful for treating the throat, larynx and vocal cords. It is also known to help balance the metabolism, boost your immune system and even aid digestive disorders, specifically in those who suffer with calcium deficiencies. It is said that Sodalite can help lower blood pressure and stimulate the absorption of body fluids. Sodalite is a great crystal to keep in the workplace as it boosts feelings of self-esteem and self-trust whilst combatting electromagnetic radiation coming from your technological gadgets that leave your mind feeling a little fuzzy! Not only does its calming vibration cool down hot tempers, it can also help cool down fevers. I always reach for my Sodalite when I'm feeling burnt out and have lots of racing thoughts – I simply hold it in my hands while taking deep breaths for roughly thirty seconds and it always does the trick!

CLEAR QUARTZ

◇◇◇◇◇◇◇

If there is one healing crystal that you need to know about – it's Clear Quartz. This powerhouse crystal is the most powerful healing and energy amplifying stone on the planet. It is the stone of the sun, health and happiness. Known as the 'master healer', Quartz absorbs energy from sunlight and the life force in plants, trees and flowers which it will store and concentrate so this energy can be released and used for healing or magic. This stone instils a sense of optimism and clear purpose. It also absorbs negativity from the atmosphere and transforms it into rays of healing. This crystal is very powerful at channelling and unblocking energies, revitalizing the body on a physical, mental, emotional and spiritual level. As well as stimulating the immune system and bringing the body into balance, it also aids functioning of the organs. It is a fabulous stone for those who struggle with their memory and concentration, making it a must-have for anyone studying for exams. It is also helpful for students because of its ability to draw off negative energy and neutralize background radiation. This crystal helps aid all the chakras, bringing your inner universe back into alignment so you can step into your true power!

TIP FOR HEALING

Use Clear Quartz for a powerful healing bath! First, cleanse the space with lavender and light a candle for each corner of the bath. Once it's ready, add a piece of Clear Quartz to it and let its amazing properties get to work whilst enjoying a relaxing soak.

ANGELITE

✧✧✧✧✧✧✧

This glacier-blue and lilac ancient Peruvian healing stone alleviates suffering and transmutes pain into the process of rebirth and healing. Angelite is known for being an amazing healer of the physical body, and has been reported to help relieve headaches, heal diseases and aid weight loss by regulating fluid balances. Not only that, it also works wonders at renewing blood vessels and certainly has beneficial properties related to the heart. This beautiful pale stone raises the state of conscious awareness, connecting you with your higher self and spirit guides/angels. It enhances psychic healing and enables astral travel and spiritual journeys. If you haven't heard of the term 'astral travel' before, then allow me to explain. Astral travel is a practice which allows people to have spiritual, out-of-body experiences intentionally. Angelite is said to have many emotional healing benefits such as helping us work through feelings of anger and anxiety, rather than letting them sit in the body and manifest into illness. As well as dispelling these negative feelings, it helps you speak your truth and attract tranquillity into your life. Angelite encourages peace, sensitivity and kindness whilst protecting the environment and the body. With its connection to the Throat Chakra, this stone is particularly useful for those needing assistance in bringing balance to their thyroid gland or those suffering with a throat infection.

BLUE AVENTURINE

◇◇◇◇◇◇◇◇

If you are trying to release destructive patterns of behaviour that are preventing you from stepping into the best version of yourself, this is the stone for you! This mystical, dark-blue crystal is wonderful at balancing emotions. It assists us in taking a calm approach to external stressful situations and, therefore, brings about a sense of inner peace. It is wonderful for those who feel stagnant in their energy. It enhances our inner masculine energy, allowing us to take leadership in our life, confidently make decisions, empower our inner strength and encourage self-discipline. Because of this, it is also perfect for anyone suffering from self-destructive habits such as smoking, overeating and substance abuse. As well as this, Blue Aventurine helps bring out our psychic abilities and strengthens our intuition by clearing the Throat and Third Eye Chakra. The amount of healing properties Blue Aventurine comes in handy for is quite remarkable. This crystal is associated with the general health of bones, teeth and the absorption of necessary minerals, and also targets problems in the ears, oesophagus and the parathyroid glands. If you seek assistance in regulating your hormones, Blue Aventurine is a must-have! It is said that it can assist individuals struggling to conceive, those going through hormonal treatment and even just that good old time of the month! It has properties that reinforce the arterial walls and strengthen both the respiratory and circulatory systems. If you struggle with your mental focus, Blue Aventurine can help you concentrate. I particularly love this stone's use for those with ADHD because of its assistance with hyperactivity and mental focus. This 'does-it-all' stone also helps treat common colds, ease facial tics, physical pains, chronic stiffness, muscle twitches and spasms. Because of its connection with the Throat Chakra, it can also assist those who struggle with speech impediments.

SELENITE

◊◊◊◊◊◊◊

This soothing and mystical crystal is named after Selene, the Greek goddess of the full moon. This stone is especially unique as it can be used to effectively cleanse other crystals of negative energy and charge them back to their original vibrational state. Selenite is amazing for fertility, pregnancy and motherhood journeys by protecting the health of the mother and child. I love Selenite for emotional healing due to its powerful ability to cleanse the aura. Every evening I will cleanse my body's energetic field using my trusty Selenite wand. Selenite wands are literally what they sound like – a wand made of Selenite. However, often these wands are actually made of Satin Spar which is a variety of gypsum similar to Selenite. Given that Selenite and Satin Spar are so popular for clearing negative energies, a simple way you can work with a Selenite or Satin Spar wand is by sweeping the body free from any unwanted energies at the end of a stressful day!

RUBY ZOISITE

◇◇◇◇◇◇◇

This unique stone is a combination of two magical, healing crystals and is also known as Ruby in Zoisite. If you are drawn to this stone, it may be a nudge from your spirit guides to express your individuality and embrace your inner free spirit. It is great for healing a broken heart and calms excess emotional reactions. This is due to its association with both the Heart and the Root Chakra. Ruby Zoisite also channels enthusiasm into positive action whilst amplifying feelings of joy and spontaneity. As well as this, this crystal will assist you in your magical journey by encouraging visualizations and imagination. It is said that Ruby Zoisite can help protect its user against viruses and infections. Another healing benefit of this stone is boosting fertility. Known as 'the stone of gratitude', it can help to relieve feelings of grief, anger and despair whilst reminding us to take care of ourselves. This stone boosts feelings of happiness and appreciation for all that you have in your life, and a happy, healthy mind is the key to unlocking your true potential!

TIP FOR HEALING

My personal favourite way to welcome healing energy into my life is by incorporating crystals, such as Ruby Zoisite, into my jewellery. Whether it is a bracelet, a necklace or even a ring, having this crystal directly against your skin will allow the healing properties to connect with your body!

SMOKY QUARTZ

◇◇◇◇◇◇◇

You will hear me mention Smoky Quartz a lot throughout this book and that is because I just love it so much. It is a crystal that presented itself to me later on in my journey when I really needed it, and its effects have been transformational for me. If you resonate with my former mindset, I know you will love Smoky Quartz too. Do you find yourself stuck in negative situations or thought patterns that no longer serve you? Are you ready to release all that is holding you back energetically from living a life that's in alignment with your highest, happiest self? Then this is the crystal for you. It is a grounding stone known for its ability to help you move on from difficult or painful experiences by guiding you to a higher state of being. It is also a highly protective stone and removes negative or unwanted energy. Use Smoky Quartz as a gentle, healing force that grounds you and provides the energetic stability you need when life gets chaotic. Smoky Quartz is also known to have many beneficial healing properties such as healing the cells of the body, assisting the fluid systems in the body, improving skin tone and increasing the capacity the body has to absorb calcium.

TIP FOR HEALING

Use Smoky Quartz to unstick yourself from negative situations and thought patterns that no longer serve you!

---

chapter 4.

CRYSTALS FOR TRANSFORMATION

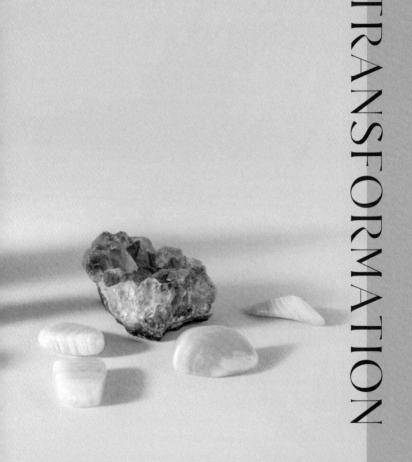

CRYSTALS FOR TRANSFORMATION & CONFIDENCE

Unlocking your power and stepping into the best possible version of yourself starts with your inner dialogue – or how you talk to yourself. We all talk to ourselves all day every day – interpreting events or telling ourselves stories about what happened in the past or might happen in the future. How kind we are to ourselves will reflect in the decisions we make, what we attract into our lives and, most importantly, how we feel inside. I am not naturally a confident person. I was very shy growing up and still struggle with social anxiety. However, since incorporating crystals into my daily life I have truly grown into someone I am proud to be.

When I was at school, I remember doing everything in my power to portray a version of myself that was totally false, purely because I felt I would be more accepted by my peers. Every action I took, every word out of my mouth, the way I styled my hair, wore my makeup was determined by other people's perception of me. This is probably due to the fact I was bullied by a group of girls at my school when I was 10/11 years old. This particular group of girls were actually who I would have called my 'best friends' at the time, but you know how school can be – pretty much overnight they turned on me and decided I was now 'not cool enough' to be their friend.

I want to make something clear: I have no resentment towards these girls; I certainly was no saint at school. I've been bullied and I've been the bully at certain points in my life, and I have learnt in my adult life that people are always just doing their best with the level of consciousness they had at that time. More importantly, I've learnt that hurt people do exactly that – hurt people. When I went into secondary school I wanted a fresh start, so I began to observe other people's behaviour and how others responded to this behaviour, and this ultimately formed my 'new identity'. The smart, kind girl who excelled at school and always tried in lessons became a gobby, disrespectful delinquent who caused havoc in classrooms and pretended she didn't even know how to spell her own name. I refer to 'her' in the third person because this image I was trying to portray was definitely a stranger to me. I would throw shoes at teachers, I wore my 'most detentions in the year' title like a badge of honour and, worst of all, I picked on other students who I actually quite admired. Even if they were considered 'uncool', at least they had the nerve to be true to themselves, a skill I did not master until a lot later on in life. Although I am not proud of this time of my life, I forgive myself for it. Like I said earlier, people can only do their best with the level of consciousness they had at that time. To truly love and accept ourselves for who we are, we also have to acknowledge the mistakes we have made along the way, embrace the lessons we have learnt from those mistakes and use them as fuel for positive change.

I now know exactly who I am, and I'm proud of that person. Whatever transformation you feel needs to take place in your life, whether it be mind, body or spirit, crystals can help you. In this chapter I will guide you through my top crystals for feeling like the best version of yourself as well as the most important things I learnt on my own confidence journey. Please know that if I took myself from a dark place to becoming a happier, more confident person – anyone can! And incorporating crystals into my daily life turbocharged the changes I wanted to make. In this chapter I'll explain how you can make changes too.

DARK FEMININE ENERGY

You may have already heard the term 'Dark Feminine Energy' but let's talk about how we can use it to feel like the most confident, bad-bitch version of ourselves. Let's get one thing straight, dark feminine energy isn't to be confused with light feminine energy which is more softly spoken, nurturing and sometimes naive. Dark feminine is magnetic, highly intuitive, powerful and, as you may have guessed, dark. Light feminine energy, also known as divine feminine energy, is the side of a woman that is loving and nurturing. If you picture the typical maternal, compassionate image of a woman, that is the light side of femininity. As women we are encouraged to display these traits and I'm certainly not saying that being in tune with our light feminine energy is a bad thing. What I am saying is when we embrace and embody both our inner light and dark energy, that is where our true power lies, and crystals are a great tool to help us connect to both sides of our feminine energy.

The first thing to understand is that your dark feminine side is not really encouraged by society. Centuries of patriarchy have suppressed feminine power. The patriarchal system is based on superiority and control rather than compassion, and the very way in which it functions is by suppressing traits of feminine energy such as patience and emotional understanding. Masculine energy is logical, direct, and yearns to conquer, whereas feminine energy is more creative and emotional. This 'emotional' womanly trait is commonly mistaken as being the overly sensitive, crying at *Love Actually* kind of emotional, so often, as women, we hide this side of ourselves so as to avoid being judged. When you access your inner dark feminine goddess you are accessing your shadow self where you suppress a lot of emotions. Because of social conditioning, the shadow self feeds off feelings of shame and guilt that have been instilled in us our whole lives and without realizing, a lot of us are reinforcing our own prisons. Since we were little, we have had it drilled into us to behave a certain way, express our emotions a certain way and even to look a certain way. To be in your dark feminine energy is to free yourself from the shackles of shame and regret by running towards these uncomfortable emotions rather than away from them. You are embracing your perceived 'flaws', being fully authentic and not hiding or suppressing anything. As a result, those in their dark feminine energy are able to articulate their needs and desires effectively. This is because they know their worth and will act accordingly. If you are ready to step into your power, crystals are a potent way to assist you in entering your dark feminine era. So let's explore the key elements to embodying the dark feminine and how crystals can help you.

132

Are there any sides to your personality that you try to keep hidden? Why?

....
....
....
....
....
....
....
....
....
....
....
....
....
....
....
....

BOUNDARIES

The number one tip to unlock your dark feminine energy is setting clear boundaries. Dark feelings often stem from the fear of our needs not being met. When we suppress these emotions, we are being inauthentic to our souls and, as a result, abandoning our own needs. This is the opposite of dark feminine. By honouring your core desires and needs you will activate your dark feminine, and actually start getting what you want! If someone doesn't like your boundaries, that says a hell of a lot more about them than it does about you. And I can promise you, from personal experience, it is far easier to adjust your life to their absence than it is to adjust your boundaries to their disrespect. Setting healthy boundaries isn't about keeping people separate from you. It's about choosing and articulating how you are willing, and not willing, to be treated. And here's a concept that I struggled with for a very long time but now couldn't live without – IT IS OKAY TO SAY NO. Even if you are letting someone down. If you are protecting your peace, it is okay to say no! If you know a place, a person or a situation is going to drain you of your energy in a negative way, it is okay to say NO. The majority of us grew up believing that we are responsible for other people's feelings. Or that bending over backwards to our

CRYSTALS FOR TRANSFORMATION ◆

own detriment just so that people feel more comfortable is a way of showing love. I'm telling you now, it's not. Respect your mind, your body and your soul, set some boundaries!

I know this is easier said than done. Believe me – when I first attempted to set some boundaries it felt like I was speaking an entirely new language. When I was a teenager, I had a certain group of friends that would overstep each others' boundaries constantly. Specifically when we would go out drinking, the way we interacted with each other wasn't far off feral. I was certainly not innocent in this either – a few Jägerbombs and I suddenly thought I was Mike Tyson. But no matter how messy the arguments got between our girl group, we always apologized and asserted our boundaries with each other the next day and promised to never behave like that with each other again. This was a cycle that repeated throughout my entire college experience and, as a result, in my adult life I always shied away from setting boundaries as the past had taught me that doing so was just a waste of my breath. These girls and I are friends again now, but it's safe to say we had a lot of growing up to do. The point I'm making is that setting boundaries is useless unless you uphold them, and this is something that comes with practice.

I've always been drawn to very opinionated women, and the way to have positive, healthy friendships is to have mutual respect for each other and each others' boundaries. My sisters are like my best friends and we are all very strong characters, but we have no problem effectively communicating how we feel and respecting each others' opinions and boundaries. This is also true with the group of strong, independent girls that I would call my best friends. We have all grown up together and are constantly having to set new boundaries with each other as we have entered different phases in our lives. A massive issue we always respect is phone communication. In the age of multiple WhatsApp group chats for every single group of friends, event, or even planning someone's birthday present, I think we can all agree our phones can become a source of overwhelming stress. When my friends and I were younger, we would get annoyed and take it personally if someone didn't reply at the speed of light. But as we've grown and everyone's lives have changed so much, we all have new responsibilities or relationships that demand more of our attention and each of us at some time has had to set a boundary that we will catch up with each other in our own time. And I promise you if you are reading this and you have set a boundary with a friend who continues to disrespect this boundary, they are not a friend. If you are struggling to imagine what setting a boundary would even sound like, I will share my top examples of assertive boundaries as well as my favourite crystals to help you.

'Respect your mind, your body, and your soul by setting some boundaries.'

'I care about your
feelings but I don't appreciate
the way you are expressing
them to me right now.'

'I refuse to continue in a
conversation where I'm not
being heard.'

'We either talk about
this respectfully or we
don't talk about it at all.'

'I will not compromise
my feelings for your
comfort.'

'I am not asking you to
evaluate my emotions – how
I feel is not up for debate.'

'I am not going to put my
energy into a situation where
it's not reciprocated.'

'Do you think I let
everyone treat me this way,
or just you?'

'If you cannot hold space
for my emotions I can
happily hold the door for
you on your way out.'

Amazonite

<small>◇◇◇◇◇◇◇</small>

Known as 'the stone of courage', by its very nature this stone helps you stand up for what you believe is important and take the rightful place as the main character in your story. Amazonite works with the Heart and Throat Chakras, allowing you to speak your truth with ease. Keeping a level head when setting boundaries is very helpful and Amazonite is a very soothing stone that reduces anger and irritability, aligning the physical body with the etheric (your aura). This stone also helps you combat fear of judgement and confrontation.

Blue Aventurine

<small>◇◇◇◇◇◇◇</small>

This mystical, dark-blue crystal is wonderful at balancing emotions. It assists us in taking a calm approach to external stressful situations and therefore is a wonderful helping hand when it comes to setting boundaries. It enhances our inner masculine energy, allowing us to take leadership in our life, confidently make decisions, empower our inner strength and encourage self-discipline. As well as this, Blue Aventurine helps bring out our psychic abilities and strengthens our intuition by clearing the Throat and Third Eye Chakras. When you work with Blue Aventurine, you will be in tune with your needs and will be able to vocalize them with confidence.

Are there any boundaries you need to set in your life going forward to protect your peace?

....
....
....
....
....
....
....
....
....
....
....
....
....
....

SELF-CONCEPT

Honestly, working on your sense of self-concept is the key to stepping into your true power. Your self-concept is simply how you see yourself; it's a collection of beliefs you hold to be true about yourself. Your self-concept ultimately defines your level of self-confidence. When you see yourself as the ultimate prize and know deeply that you are worthy of all you desire, your manifestations will come to you with ease. You will also attract other people, situations and opportunities that meet you at that same high-level loving frequency. So let me share with you my top practices and crystals to improve your-self concept.

Reflection journaling

This practice is wonderful for improving your internal self-concept. First, grab a pen and paper. Then write down at least ten things that you like about your personality. Are you especially nurturing or caring towards others? Do you have a great sense of humour? Are you someone who is particularly motivated and goal driven? Write these down as statements, for example, 'I am caring,' 'I am fun to be around,' etc. Holding your favourite confidence crystal whilst doing this is a great way to amplify the energy.

Make a Self-Love Plan

Grab yourself a fresh sheet of paper and split it into four sections. Then title each section 'health', 'wealth', 'soul' and 'love'. You're

1. ....
   ....
2. ....
   ....
3. ....
   ....
4. ....
   ....
5. ....
   ....
6. ....
   ....
7. ....
   ....
8. ....
   ....
9. ....
   ....
10. ....
   ....

then going to work through each section focusing on where you can offer yourself some more self-love in each one of these areas of your life. For example, with health, are you drinking enough water? Have you eaten anything green in the past twenty-four hours? Because I know I haven't. And with soul, when was the last time you meditated? Are there certain things you are overthinking that you need to deal with? Just work through each section strategically and see what pops up!

How could I be offering myself more love in these areas?

Health	Wealth

Soul	Love

Confidence Playlist

Music is a seriously underestimated tool for manifesting anything you want into your life, especially confidence. I honestly believe that music is medicine for the soul. I want you to put together a playlist of bad-bitch confidence anthems. Just put together all your favourite songs that make you feel like THAT girl! And you are going to start listening to this playlist regularly. By doing this, you are going to start reprogramming that subconscious of yours that this is the energy you want to radiate. Here is a sample playlist of ten songs I put on whenever I need to give myself a confidence boost:

'Started' by Iggy Azalea

'Goddess Code' by Lizzy Jeff

'7 Rings' by Ariana Grande

'Therefore I Am' by Billie Eilish

'All I Do Is Win' by DJ Khaled

'Confetti' by Little Mix and Saweetie

'Daisy' by Ashnikko

'Boss Bitch' by Doja Cat

'Woman' by Kesha

'Rockstar 101' by Rihanna

Confidence Affirmations

As mentioned in previous chapters, programming your crystals with intentions is a practice I find extremely powerful. So grab yourself a crystal with properties that boost feelings of self-confidence such as Honey Calcite, Carnelian or Red Jasper. Hold it to your chest and say some confidence-boosting affirmations. You can do this aloud or in your head, but I personally find speaking them aloud really helps you feel and embody this energy. If you don't know where to start or what to say, see the opposite page for some of my favourite confidence affirmations.

Hypnosis

This tip is simple but effective. Alongside affirmations, healing involving awareness of our inner child and shadow self, hypnosis is another method I love to use for reprogramming the subconscious mind. The subconscious mind is most susceptible to new information when it is in that half-awake hypnosis state. Hypnosis and meditation are both trance states that result in similar brain-wave patterns. Hypnosis uses the guidance of a therapist or experienced professional, whereas meditation is usually done independently. This is why sleep meditations and hypnosis are incredible at rewiring the subconscious brain and you can find loads online specifically aimed at confidence. I personally love all of Iris Dailey's hypnoses which you can find on her website (www.irisdailey.com). You can amplify it further by sleeping with a confidence crystal under your pillow. Avoid sleeping with energising crystals though, as they can disrupt your rest!

'I am way too
full of life to
play small.'

'My
energy is
irresistible.'

'I radiate
confidence.'

'I am worthy
of all that is
good in this
universe.'

'I deserve
the best and I
accept the
best now.'

HONEY CALCITE

✧✧✧✧✧✧✧

This stone of confidence is, in my opinion, seriously underrated. Honey Calcite is exceptional at assisting us in stepping into a position of personal power. It encourages responsibility in leadership and can help with recovering from abusive situations. It does this by increasing feelings of self-worth, empowerment and courage whilst working with our Sacral and Solar Plexus Chakras. Honey Calcite also works with our Crown Chakra, moving divine energy from the Crown Chakra all the way down to the Root Chakra, raising our vibration and amplifying positive energy so we can continue on our journey of self-discovery.

RED JASPER

✧✧✧✧✧✧✧

This stone increases self-confidence, self-trust, emotional protection and courage. Because Red Jasper is an energetic stabilizer, it helps you to let go of people or habits that are no longer serving you. It will also help you stand in your power and have the confidence to remain true to yourself. According to Viking legend, the handle of the sword of Siegfried the dragon-slayer was made with Red Jasper to give him courage. So if you are ready to unleash your inner dragon-slayer then work with this stone and its courageous, passionate energies!

CARNELIAN

◇◇◇◇◇◇◇

Are you ready to radiate goddess energy, step into your power and claim your inner confidence? If so, Carnelian is the stone for you. Associated with the Solar Plexus Chakra, this gorgeous burnt-orange stone will remind you of your unique strengths, filling you with courage whilst removing feelings of doubt and despair. Carnelian is, above all, a crystal of personal happiness and fulfilment – it will act as a shield from attempted psychic intrusion into your thoughts. It will also bring out your brave side and encourage you to take action towards your goals and to never accept treatment from others that is less than you deserve.

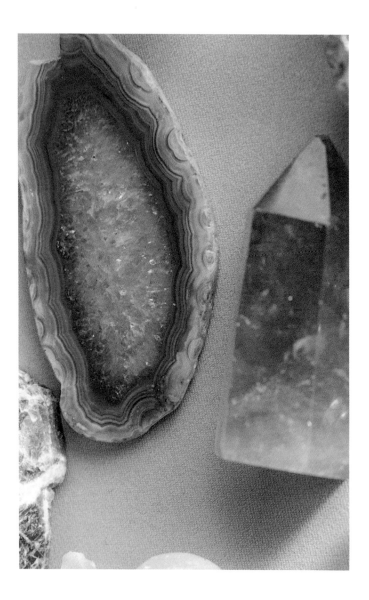

ADAPTING TO CHANGE AND MASTERING THE ART OF DETACHMENT

The art of detachment is the process of disconnecting from certain things that may be hindering our own positive transformation. To put it simply, detachment can be summed up by the phrase 'it is what it is'. As human beings, we are conditioned by society to work towards goals rather than to enjoy the process of obtaining those goals. The art of detachment is a concept that did not come naturally to me at all at first. As I said in chapter one, I have an anxious attachment style. Because of this, when I get attached to a person, I get SERIOUSLY attached. I did not adapt well to change and the thought of someone leaving my life was soul-crushing. This meant that I held on to negative people, patterns of behaviour, situations and even jobs far longer than I should have. To master the art of detachment is to accept you have no control and, therefore, should not stress over factors that are out of your control. Once I realized that the way I was clinging on to these things that were not serving me was hindering my personal growth, I made it my mission to become a master of detachment. I did this through using crystals that are known for speeding up personal positive transformation and I programmed them all with the same intention. The intention I set for these crystals has, I would argue, been the most powerful affirmation I have ever used:

'I do not chase, I attract. What belongs to me will simply find me. Anything that is meant for me will not pass me by.'

Every day I would say this affirmation out loud to my crystals and carry them with me. The results were extraordinary! At first, it felt like my world was falling apart. I lost my job and a lot of people suddenly left my life. At the time I couldn't grasp why this was all happening to me but now, looking back, it's very simple. The universe heard my request and was simply making room for better. By holding on to these things I had outgrown, I was blocking myself from the very things I actually desired. Working with these crystals amplified all the negative blocks that needed removing and, ultimately, helped remove them from my life. After this, I started my business, met some amazing new people, started feeling the happiest I've ever felt and now here I am, writing this book! If you are ready to accomplish the true heights of what you can achieve, detach from things that are of less importance and embark on your journey of positive transformation, these are the crystals for you.

MALACHITE

◇◇◇◇◇◇◇

Known as 'the stone of transformation', Malachite encourages positive change in your life. It helps you see clearly what is blocking your spiritual growth, whilst drawing out deep feelings and allowing you to break patterns that do not serve your highest purpose. Also referred to as 'the stone of protection' because it absorbs negative energies and pollutants from the atmosphere and from the body. Malachite is an extremely powerful crystal and should only be used when polished, as its raw form can be toxic due to the high levels of copper it contains. If you are ready for tough love for your greatest good, this is the stone for you.

SERAPHINITE

◇◇◇◇◇◇◇

Ready for some real change in your life? Let me introduce you to 'the high vibration stone'. It really lives up to its name and is hands down one of the strongest crystals you can come into contact with and can drastically alter your life. It will massively heighten your intuition and intellect, whilst allowing you to maintain a clear and level head, and to deeply reflect upon the current situations in your life and assess which of those may no longer serve you on your life path. You will have a strengthened connection to your higher self and gain clarity regarding your true desires. Seraphinite pushes you into an accelerated growth cycle where your soul takes the lead

instead of your mind and heart. Your soul is the true embodiment of your consciousness and it will constantly show you your true wants and needs. Let this stone take you on a journey of self-discovery, awakening and transformation.

BLACK RAINBOW MOONSTONE

⬦⬦⬦⬦⬦⬦⬦

This beautiful crystal is often connected to the planet Venus, making it perfect for those looking to connect with their divine feminine energy. Due to its association with the moon, Black Rainbow Moonstone represents rebirth and assists you in starting a new cycle in your life. An amazing stone for stepping into your power and gaining inner confidence, it radiates protective vibrations that stabilize our emotions so that they cannot be influenced by others. If you find that other people's toxic energy or opinions are hindering your own personal growth, this gem is perfect for you.

AMETHYST

⬦⬦⬦⬦⬦⬦⬦

Amethyst is the stone of spirituality. It is well known for assisting in meditations, finding spiritual contentment and fulfilling inner peace. This high-vibrational stone works with its user on a mental level by relieving stress but also opening up spiritual awareness and intuition. It is known for working with the Crown Chakra, which is the chakra responsible for opening you up to unlimited truth and connecting you with your highest, best self. This gorgeous, purple gem is a powerful tool for attracting tranquillity, quietening the mind and, therefore, allowing you to access your inner wisdom.

YOUR INTUITION

I get asked a lot what it actually means and looks like to connect with, and trust, your intuition. Intuitive abilities aren't just for psychics and the Mystic Meg types you see with their crystal balls. We all have intuition; however, some are more strongly connected to it than others. So what exactly is your intuition? And how do you strengthen your connection to it? Put simply, your intuition is your ability to instinctively understand, without need for conscious reasoning. We all use our intuition on a daily basis. You know that gut feeling you get when you know something just doesn't seem right? Bingo, that's your intuition. Or when you experience excitement over a certain opportunity? Again, that's your intuition. Our intuition is related to our highest self and is always trying to direct us on to our soul's path. However, the intuition is often confused with the ego. The main difference between the two is that your intuition lives in the present, so it will never give you an explanation about why it feels the way that it does. It is your soul communicating with you, and when you feel a nudge from your intuition you can't always explain why you feel that way – you just do! Whereas with your ego, it will try and predict the future because it wants control of the outcome. As we discussed in chapter two, your ego is often just trying to protect you. Because of this your ego will make up stories in your head about why you should or shouldn't do something purely so it can keep you in your comfort zone.

When I first started connecting with my intuition I felt a strong intuitive pull to create a TikTok account to talk about all things crystals, spirituality and mindset. However, my ego was telling me that this was a silly idea, that it would be super cringy and no one would want to watch it. For a long time I battled with both sides, unsure which was my intuition and which was my ego. But months went by and this nudge to make a TikTok account didn't go away, so I bit the bullet and made the account. I knew it was my intuition because I had no idea what the outcome was going to be – I was doing it purely because I felt like I wanted to. And now here I am with 21.5 million likes on my TikTok videos and nearly a million followers. Moral of the story, your ego lies to you in an attempt to protect you, whereas your intuition is always trying to align you with your highest purpose.

Connecting to and trusting your intuition is crucial for your self-confidence, because by connecting to our intuition we learn to trust in ourselves and our intuitive abilities. We can then stop seeking validation from others and feel confident that the choices we make are right for us, no matter what anyone else thinks. When we begin to intentionally develop our intuition it's like building a muscle; it takes time, patience and practice. Human emotions such as stress, fear and doubt can block us from our intuition, so it's important not to be hard on yourself if developing your intuitive skills is all new to you! Crystals are an excellent tool for connecting you with your intuition, so let me share with you my favourite crystals to help strengthen your intuitive abilities:

LABRADORITE

◇◇◇◇◇◇

Known as 'the stone of magic', Labradorite is amazing for self-discovery and awakening your awareness of your inner spirit and psychic abilities – bringing your magical powers to the surface. This beautiful iridescent crystal is amazing at enhancing your intuition because it elevates your consciousness and puts you in dialogue with your highest self.

LAPIS LAZULI

◇◇◇◇◇◇

This stone was known by Ancient Egyptians as 'the stone of the gods', due to not only its starry-sky-like heavenly appearance but also its ability to unite the different aspects of ourselves and our lives to create harmony of mind, body and spirit. If you are struggling to connect with your intuition, Lapis Lazuli is the stone for you. This is because it works on the upper chakras including the Throat, Third Eye and Crown Chakras, unlocking the door to higher consciousness and stimulating your psychic abilities.

THE POWER OF FEMININE ARCHETYPES

All feminine archetypes are based on Jungian psychology and research into the inner lives of some of history's most fascinating women. These archetypes are recurring patterns identified by psychologist Carl Jung that manifest themselves across society. According to Jung, understanding our archetype allows us to fundamentally understand the foundation of our unlearned, instinctive patterns of behaviour. The benefit of identifying your feminine archetype is that you will then have a greater understanding of what brings you joy, what challenges you may face, as well as knowledge of your strongest attributes and how to use them to your advantage. When you embody the characteristics of your specific archetype, you are authentically, unapologetically you and your aura becomes magnetic. This is because, like many of the other self-love techniques I've talked about in this book, confidence is about understanding yourself. More importantly, self-confidence is about accepting yourself, flaws and all.

After finding out your archetype, you can use certain crystals that will work with and amplify the energy that this specific archetype embodies. It is important to keep in mind that though you have one main archetype, you can relate to and resemble multiple archetypes. And that's great! Women are multidimensional, versatile individuals, and we can learn to confidently use these strengths to our advantage! So let's get to it.

The Venus

This particular archetype is very powerful. The energy of a Venus woman is magnetic and mysterious. Someone with this archetype embodies dark feminine energy and embraces their sensuality. Venuses are quietly confident and exude erotic yet classy vibes. When a Venus walks into a room, all eyes are on her. Her spontaneous, fiery energy is both her power and her downfall. Red Jasper is the perfect crystal to help balance a Venus energy whilst allowing her to thrive in her vibrant, sexual energy.

The Mischief

165

FAMOUS MISCHIEF ARCHETYPE: **Janet Jackson**

Those who embody this archetype are openly connected with their inner child. Their playful, mischievous charm makes them intriguing to all they come into contact with. Mischief women's child-like charisma should not be confused with naive or immature behaviour. They are warm, compassionate and possess the ability to be free with their emotions. Sunstone will work beautifully for any Mischief female looking to embrace her captivating qualities. Sunstone showers all areas of your life with joy, just as a Mischief showers all those she meets with joy.

The Cherie

The icon of the archetypes and, if I do say so myself, the one I relate to most. A sweet concoction of girlish charm and womanly sensuality, Cherie women have a natural charm that makes them irresistible. Unapologetically themselves, they have the bravery to say and do things other people wouldn't. They maintain a daring and bold energy whilst being soft and compassionate at the same time. For those with this archetype I would recommend Amazonite. This stone will allow them to continue confidently speaking their truth and to step into their power whilst balancing any conflicting emotions that may be hindering them.

The Temptress

FAMOUS TEMPTRESS ARCHETYPE: **Catherine Tramell in**
Basic Instinct

If there is any archetype that is most likely to break your heart, it's the Temptress. Temptress women possess the ability to withdraw, retreat and distance themselves emotionally at any given moment. They are highly independent and prioritize freedom. Their appeal lies in their 'I don't need anyone but myself' attitude and this archetype certainly doesn't shy away from speaking her mind. I would recommend Rhodonite to those with this archetype because it will continue to encourage the prioritization of self-love. However, Rhodonite will also allow them to open their hearts to others, which can often be a challenge for a Temptress woman.

The Duchess

FAMOUS DUCHESS ARCHETYPE: **Ayesha Curry**

The Duchess radiates down-to-earth, warm energy. She exudes vulnerability and possesses the ability to connect with others on a very deep level. Those with this archetype don't do surface-level relationships and cannot fake their emotions. Highly empathetic, the Duchess archetypes always search for the best in people and their power is rooted in their nurturing persona. A challenge they may face is giving themselves the same love they openly give to others. Because of this I would recommend Amethyst, the all-healing stone that encourages those who use it to give themselves the love they need to allow their energy to flow again. This crystal also helps to relieve feelings of sadness and grief, and if anyone is able to feel emotion at its deepest level it's the Duchess!

The Cosmopolite

FAMOUS COSMOPOLITE ARCHETYPE: **Dominique Deveraux in *Dynasty***

Similar to the Venus, the Cosmopolite carries herself with a sensual energy, but a Cosmopolite's true power lies with her wit and charm. Graceful, elegant and dignified at all times, the Cosmopolite uses her charms strategically. These women have high standards, as they should! However, their perfectionism, and sometimes judgemental thoughts, can be their downfall. Labradorite is an excellent stone for this archetype. It will inspire their creative energy whilst quieting an overactive mind, bringing the best out of them.

The Queen

FAMOUS QUEEN ARCHETYPE: **Beyoncé**

Natural-born leaders, Queens have an unforgettable regal presence that demands attention. Those with this archetype are cautious with their energy and will not waste it on anything they do not view as worthy. When in love, Queens are fiercely loyal but at the end of the day it will always be their way or the highway! They will always lean towards the finer things in life and exude glamour. Sometimes their possessive, jealous and competitive nature can get the better of them, so for Queens I recommend Citrine. This crystal shields against spite and jealousy whilst encouraging their inner light! Queens are also very goal orientated and, as the stone of abundance, Citrine will assist them in succeeding.

The Gypsy

FAMOUS GYPSY ARCHETYPE: **Carrie Bradshaw in *Sex and the City***

Gypsies are unbothered by the opinions of others. They are connected with their own mind and body, meaning they don't let people in easily. Gypsy ladies are free-spirited yet entirely self-sufficient, and the time taken trying to figure her out adds to her appeal. She is a mystery that people want to solve and her devil-may-care attitude is enticing. Because of her ability to cut off from emotional vulnerability, it can be hard for the Gypsy woman to forge real connections. Pink Tourmaline is great for those with this archetype as it encourages compassion, allowing love to flow.

The Hedonist

FAMOUS HEDONIST ARCHETYPE: **Sophia Loren**

The presence of this archetype is intoxicating and addictive. They possess a warm, affectionate energy and their 'live-in-the-moment' mindset is infectious. Hedonist women are outgoing, comfortable in their own skins, and use their confidence to uplift those around them. For these seductive, light-hearted individuals I would recommend Carnelian. This crystal aligns beautifully with their energy, amplifying their sensual energy and nurturing their carefree nature. It will also allow them to continue showing up as the most confident version of themselves!

The Muse

FAMOUS MUSE ARCHETYPE: **Lana Del Rey**

The presence of the Muse is so captivating it almost feels like they are from a different planet! Those with this archetype have a soulful yet calm demeanour and are able to connect deeply with themselves spiritually. They are naturally introverted but their magnetic energy means they do not go unnoticed. Muse women have many admirers but this doesn't affect their down-to-earth, grounded energy. A challenge for Muse women may be that their internal focus leaves them feeling cut off from their sensual, spontaneous side. Smoky Quartz is a must-have for Muse women. It will help them see that sexuality is normal and healthy, and it will allow them to comfortably explore their sexual energy. Also, this crystal is aligned with the Root Chakra which is responsible for grounding. Being grounded is a strength of the Muse, so this crystal will help them hold true to their own authentic power.

The Fairy

FAMOUS FAIRY ARCHETYPE: **Phoebe Buffay in *Friends***

Peace is top priority for Fairy women. They are comfortable being alone because they strive for contentment rather than popularity or recognition. They always have their heads in the clouds which gives them a mysterious allure that others long to figure out. Fairy women seek out magic in everything and everyone, and although they are happy alone they often yearn to feel a deep connection. Angelite would be a beautiful crystal for those with this archetype as it will strengthen their connection to their spiritual side. It will also help them speak their truth and attract the tranquillity into their life that they so desperately crave.

The Ruler

FAMOUS RULER ARCHETYPE: **Tasha St. Patrick in *Power***

These women are POWERFUL. They are masters of both feminine and masculine energy and are often a source of inspiration for others. Ruler women make amazing companions, showering their partner with attention to the point where the partner becomes completely dependent on them. Ruler women value commitment, but they also radiate a dominant queen-like energy that makes them extremely desirable. A challenge for Ruler women is giving so much in relationships that they may lose part of themselves. So for these individuals I would highly recommend Rose Quartz. This crystal radiates unconditional love and opens the Heart Chakra, playing to their strengths. But Rose Quartz will also encourage them to give this same love to themselves so they can remain confident in their own identity whilst giving love to others.

What 3 feminine archetypes do you feel like you resonate most with and why?

1. ....

....

....

2. ....

....

....

3. ....

....

....

I personally relate to the Cherie archetype the most – I even have a tattoo of Marilyn Monroe on the back of my arm! There is also a particular quote from Marilyn Monroe that I love and have always lived by: 'Imperfection is beauty, madness is genius and it's better to be absolutely ridiculous than absolutely boring.' I used to think my mix of child-like curiosity and womanly sensuality made me unbalanced and I should stick to one particular persona. Since learning about my feminine archetype, I now realize that this is in fact my superpower. Educating myself on this archetype has also helped me make sense of the Cherie's darker side, which is that because I'm so receptive to others, it can often lead me to fall into codependent, unhealthy relationships. This is why working with Amazonite has been so life-changing for me, as it helps me assert myself instead of moulding myself into a version of me that's more comfortable for somebody else. Learning to set boundaries, embrace and accept the darker sides of my identity and transform them into qualities I value has made me view myself from a new positive perspective. This improved self-concept has had a ripple effect in terms of believing I am worthy of all that I desire and also believing in my own abilities to achieve all that I desire! I find I am now far more in tune with my intuition and it's a lot easier for me to take risks because I fully trust in my own talents. Since having this shift in my self-confidence, so many more opportunities have presented themselves to me. Without self-confidence I certainly wouldn't have been brave enough to make my TikTok, start my business or write this book. If I can do it, you certainly can too!

173

chapter 5.

CRYSTALS FOR PROTECTION

CRYSTALS FOR PROTECTION

With the constant pressure and stress of everyday life, crystals are an excellent tool to ensure your environment and aura are protected. You can use crystals to physically protect certain areas such as your home and workspace, to protect yourself and your energy and also for protection when entering a new phase of your life. In this chapter we will explore all elements of crystal protection, including how I like to protect myself with crystals in all areas of my life, and my go-to crystals with specific protective properties and how to use them.

Protecting your home

Crystals have been used for centuries to ward off negative energies. Whether this be from spiritual entities or just people with bad vibes, there is a crystal that can help secure your space. If you are a homebody like me, your home is your safe haven and a place that you want to walk into and leave all negativity at the door. Crystals are perfect for this because not only do they dispel negativity, they also create a harmonious environment and even improve sleep. Because of the unique properties of each crystal, you can place them strategically around your home to amplify their benefits and vibrations. This will ensure your home remains your spiritual oasis where you can safely unwind and enjoy time alone or with loved ones. So let me share with you my favourite crystals to use around the home . . .

The Doorway

Selenite and Black Tourmaline

◇◇◇◇◇◇◇

My favourite way to ensure I'm leaving any bad vibes at the door is by keeping Selenite and Black Tourmaline at the entrance to my home. Black Tourmaline is known for its protective properties and Selenite is a powerful energy amplifier. Selenite is also wonderful at purifying anything around it, including other crystals, meaning it will be purifying my own energies as I walk through the door whilst purifying and amplifying the protective energies of the Black Tourmaline. These two powerhouse protection crystals together ensure a constant flow of good energy every time you, or any guests, enter your home. Another tip I love for anyone moving into a new home that needs redecorating is crushing Selenite in a mortar and adding it to the paint you use on your walls; this will definitely amplify harmony and healing energy whilst protecting all four walls of your home! Also, because Black Tourmaline is my go-to protective crystal, I add a piece of it to all four corners of my home to protect against all forms of negative energy.

The Kitchen

Fluorite, Carnelian, Sodalite and Rose Quartz

◇◇◇◇◇◇◇◇

I am no Nigella Lawson when it comes to the kitchen. However, I do love to use certain crystals to bring the good vibes into the kitchen to encourage me to pull out a pan every once in a while instead of ordering from the local kebab shop. Fluorite is the perfect crystal for this because it is known for keeping you on task. Which leads me nicely on to the next crystal I love to keep in my kitchen – Carnelian. This is because it is an energy-boosting crystal and I work with its energies to motivate me whilst cooking, as it is not something I naturally love to do. As you may have guessed, when it comes to brainstorming meal ideas my mind goes blank. For this I always keep Sodalite in my kitchen to amplify feelings of creativity. Sodalite is also an amazing calming crystal, which helps me to stop going full-on Gordon Ramsay mode when I inevitably burn whatever it is I'm attempting to cook. I also keep Rose Quartz in the kitchen to ensure every meal I cook is infused with loving energy and appreciation for it nurturing my body.

The Living Room

Howlite, Smoky Quartz, Hematite, Clear Quartz

∞∞∞∞∞

Howlite is my absolute favourite crystal for the home. Known as 'the home-blessing stone', it offers protection against unfriendly phantoms and encourages open, non-confrontational communication. This gorgeous white and grey stone brings increased feelings of loyalty, strength and reassurance. If you are drawn to this crystal it may be an indication from your spirit guides to slow down and touch home base for a while. You may be wondering what are spirit guides? A 'spirit guide' is a supposed non-physical being assigned to guide us to attain the greatest potential on earth. They are our personal guardian angels and assist us as we navigate life. People often try to connect with their guides through the use of crystals, tarot cards and meditation, and Howlite is a great tool for this! Howlite also encourages a peaceful night's sleep, especially for children who are afraid of the dark, so this also makes it a wonderful crystal to keep in the bedroom. Smoky Quartz is also a must-have in the living room for grounding, emotional calmness and boosting positive thoughts. Another great crystal for grounding and protecting a room from negativity is Hematite, so I keep Smoky Quartz and Hematite together with some Clear Quartz on the table in the centre of my living room. Clear Quartz works well with these two stones because it amplifies their energy and balances energy in high-traffic areas.

The Bedroom

Amazonite, Lepidolite, Amethyst, Rainbow Moonstone

◇◇◇◇◇◇◇

I like to keep particular crystals on my bedside table to promote a peaceful night's sleep. Amazonite is known for being an extremely soothing stone and will bring a tranquil vibe to your bedroom. Do you struggle with anxious thoughts racing through your mind the second you close your eyes like me? If so, I would highly recommend sleeping with some Lepidolite next to your bed. It is most known for relieving anxiety and I have personally found it has worked wonders for me! Another great stone for anxiety is Amethyst. However, I like to sleep with Amethyst under my pillow because it has properties that are specifically known to help with insomnia and nightmares so I want it as close to me as possible! Did you know that crystals can even help with recalling your dreams? It is believed that the universe sends you messages whilst you sleep that can help make sense of certain situations in your life or guide you on to your soul's path. That is why, alongside Amethyst, I also sleep with Rainbow Moonstone under my pillow because it has specific properties related to dream recall.

Carnelian, Red Jasper and Sunstone

◇◇◇◇◇◇◇

Now we have addressed the more serene setting when going to bed, it's time to address the spicier side of the bedroom. So here are the crystals I'd recommend keeping near your bed if you are trying to inject some passion into your sex life. Carnelian is exceptional at injecting a healthy dose of spice into your sex life whether you are single or wanting to rekindle the passion in an existing relationship. It is also said to aid both female fertility and male potency as well as relieving any sexual anxieties that may prevent you reaching orgasm. If you are about to have some fun adult time with your partner, pop a piece of Carnelian under each of the four corners of your mattress – thank me later! Red Jasper can also be used for increasing sexual vibrancy and passion between lovers. It is also known for increasing energy and stamina, and if you are a woman reading this book, get your man some Red Jasper jewellery, and again, thank me later. Another great crystal for this is Sunstone: it is said to increase sexual potency in men and bring happiness into all areas of your life, including your sex life!

The Bathroom

Rose Quartz, Amethyst, Clear Quartz and Ocean Jasper

◇◇◇◇◇◇◇◇

In the bathroom I would focus on keeping crystals that you can bathe with. Bathing with crystals is a powerful way to fully connect with their energy and also to relax. If you are unsure of how to create your own crystal bath, go back to chapter one; I explain it all there! Here are my favourite crystals to bathe with . . .

Having a Rose Quartz bath promotes loving energy, especially self-love. It's also said that bathing with Rose Quartz can encourage radiant, glowing skin! Amethyst is great to have in the bath because it amplifies positive energy, and helps you relax and unwind from a stressful day. I love bathing with Clear Quartz for a full healing, cleansing experience and for clarity on situations that may be bringing me confusion. Finally, Ocean Jasper is a great crystal to bathe with as it helps release negativity and regain personal power as well as encouraging self-reflection and happiness.

SPIRIT GUIDES

As I mentioned before, spirit guides, also known as spirit angels, are like our own personal guardian angels who protect us and guide us along our life path. There are six types of spirit guides; some of your personal guides will have been with you your entire life and others came into your life as and when you needed them. Think of them as your personal spiritual guidance squad! So let's talk about all of the different types of spirit guides:

Archangels

Archangels can be described as 'managers' of all the other angels. They are known as the most powerful leaders in the angel world and each archangel has a speciality . . .

ARCHANGEL RAPHAEL

Archangel Raphael's speciality is healing and the ability to work with countless humans at once. Raphael is also known to watch out for travellers, ensuring smooth transitions and safety over the course of one's journeys.

ARCHANGEL MICHAEL

Associated with the element of fire, this archangel is known to help steer individuals towards their burning passions and desires. The protector of physical, mental and emotional fitness as well as material possessions, Archangel Michael is widely regarded as the most powerful of all the archangels.

ARCHANGEL GABRIEL

Archangel Gabriel is recognized in many traditions as the female counterpart to Michael in terms of rank. This archangel rules over intuition and communication, encouraging individuals to have a better understanding of self. Connected to the element of water, Gabriel assists others by allowing them to effortlessly float through their endeavours rather than drown in their own emotions.

ARCHANGEL URIEL

This archangel is associated with the earth element and therefore helps keep humans grounded and rooted in their strength. Archangel Uriel inspires knowledge and inner wisdom and reminds those seeking his assistance that the answers are rooted within themselves.

Guardian Angels

Your guardian angels are yours and yours alone, and you can have plenty of them! Their only purpose is to assist you along your life journey and you can call on them for assistance at any time! An important point to make also, which I see a lot of people confused about, is that angels are non-denominational and work with people of all faiths and spiritual beliefs.

Spirit Animals

Yes, even your pets can join your spiritual guidance squad! If you had a pet that passed away it is highly likely they also watch over and protect you. You can also have a spirit animal because that particular animal simply embodies the traits that you may lack, and they are helping to teach you to adopt those traits. For example, if you lack courage you may have a spirit lion on your team who encourages you to find your inner roar!

Ascended Masters

These spirit guides are people that once were alive as humans and their life had deep spiritual significance, such as Buddha. Once these individuals pass away, they take their place as leaders in the spirit world and act as a guide or teacher to humans like us. These can be specific to a certain religion, but I personally believe it's a beautiful concept to imagine all ascended masters working together in harmony, no matter what culture or religion they were part of when they were alive.

Departed Loved Ones

There are plenty of stories of people sensing the energy of a loved one who has passed away still lingering in their life. It is believed that loved ones or family members who've passed can choose to join your spiritual team and help guide and support you. Whether it's a career opportunity or nurturing a relationship, your departed loved ones will always watch over you with love and care.

Helper Angels

Think of helper angels as the 'freelance workers' in your spirit team. These particular guides can pop in and out of your life when you are seeking assistance with specific situations, like making new friends or moving home. When you summon a helper angel they will stay with you until the project is completed and help guide you along the way!

Now we have gone over all the potential angels/guides in your personal spirit team (or 'spirit cheerleaders' as I like to call them) let's talk about which crystals you can use and my favourite practices to connect with them or draw on their assistance . . .

How to Meet
Your Spirit
Guides

If you are ever in a time of need you can call upon your spirit team for guidance. If you are seeking their assistance, or are simply curious to meet them, you can follow this particular ritual. Before starting, I would suggest having a notepad and pen for writing down your experience at the end of the ritual. Here is the personal way I prefer to reach out to my own spirit cheerleaders:

1. Find a quiet place where you will not be disturbed. It is important that you feel safe and comfortable in this place!

2. Hold a crystal with particular properties that relate to reaching out to the spiritual realm (I will tell you many personal favourites later on in this chapter).

3. Start quieting the mind by shifting your focus away from your own thoughts. If you are not used to meditating this can be very difficult at first so don't be hard on yourself if you don't get it straight away! I personally find it helpful to watch the light showing behind my eyelids and simply let thoughts pass over me like clouds, trying my best to not give them any attention. Another great way of shifting your focus away from your thoughts is by focusing on your breath!

4. When your mind feels settled, imagine golden beams of energy surrounding you; really feel their warmth and picture them entering your body from above, through the crown of your head and filling you up with new, healing energy.

5. Whilst this energy is flowing through you, start intentionally focusing on positive thoughts. Think of all the things you are grateful for, what you love about yourself, what you love about life, etc. Being in this high vibrational state of consciousness will allow you to be open to meeting your spirit team!

6. Now you are ready to enter your sacred garden. This is a safe space within you where you can contact your spirit guides. So imagine walking into this beautiful garden – it may feel familiar to you somehow, but the main thing to know is it is a place where you are safe and completely accepted and loved exactly as you are. Take time to walk around your personal garden and notice all its beauty and magic.

7. Once you have explored your sacred garden, you can now ask your spirit guide to come forward. When you have done this a few times you can call upon as many spirit guides as you like, but I would recommend starting with just one. When you ask them to come forward, feel excited – like you are just about to meet your best friend for the first time!

8. When your guide comes forward, feel free to have a chat with them! Ask them their name or any other questions you may have for them. You can stay in this space as long as you like.

9. When you would like to complete this ritual, thank your spirit guide for meeting you in your sacred garden and then say your goodbyes. Know that you can visit this place as often as you wish!

Notes

....

....

....

....

....

....

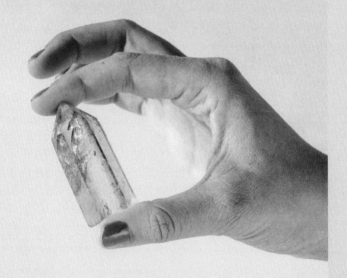

My Favourite Crystals For Connecting With My Spirit Guides

Angelite

◇◇◇◇◇◇◇◇

Angelite is an ancient Peruvian healing stone and is known for raising the state of conscious awareness, allowing you to connect with your higher self and spirit guides/angels. It enhances psychic healing and enables astral travel and spiritual journeys.

Howlite

◇◇◇◇◇◇◇◇

As I mentioned earlier in this chapter, Howlite is an amazing crystal for connecting you with your spirit guides. This is because it helps to protect your energy against unfriendly phantoms and encourages open communication with your spirit team.

Seraphinite

◇◇◇◇◇◇◇◇

This gorgeous deep-green stone is an absolute staple for me, and my go-to necklace. It is a wonderful stone for connecting you with your spirit guides. Seraphinite was even named because of its connection to the highest choir of angels, the Seraphim. It is said that using this crystal in meditation will increase a person's connection to the spiritual realm.

PROTECTING YOUR ENERGY

It is so important to protect your energy as it will determine your overall happiness as well as your motivation levels. In day-to-day life we are constantly giving away our energy. Every interaction we experience, every single person we come into contact with, will cause us to experience an energy exchange. This is because, as I discussed earlier, everything on earth is made up of an energetic vibrational frequency. Most of these energy exchanges with others we don't even notice; however, some will make you feel completely depleted of your energy. These energy exchanges can come from stressful situations, toxic people, negative conversations and certain situations that are particularly emotionally or physically draining. This can also relate to positive, new, exciting experiences. Crystals can also be used to replenish energy that has been drained from negative experiences.

Later on we will focus on how to use crystals to feel our happiest, but for now let's talk about why people's energy has such an effect on us. 'While there is no visible spark when energy is exchanged between others, a noticeable physical reaction may take place,' explains Dr Natalie Bernstein, a licensed psychologist and reiki practitioner. This is especially prevalent in individuals who are particularly sensitive or empathetic to the emotions of others. An exchange of energy takes place on an unconscious level, which can be confusing if you find it hard to separate yourself from others' energies, according to Dr Bernstein. Carrying crystals is a great way to replenish that energy.

Setting your
Intention for Protection

First, hold your chosen crystal with protection properties. Hold it to your chest and say some protection affirmations. You can do this out loud or in your head, just do what feels right to you. If you don't know where to start or what to say, let me share some of my favourite protection affirmations with you:

'I am grounded and connected to the earth and my spirit.'

'I release myself from negative feelings placed on me by others.'

'I am divinely protected.'

'My auric field is cleansed and ready to attract blessings.'

'I am protected and replenished in mind, body and soul.'

BLACK ONYX

◇◇◇◇◇◇

This crystal has immensely powerful vibrations of protection, willpower, focus and strength. Black Onyx is best known for protecting its user from negative energy. This is because it is said to absorb negativity and shield against potentially draining energy from the people and environment around you. This crystal will also work as a shield against psychic attack, which is where someone may purposely send you negative energy with harmful intentions. Not only does Black Onyx protect you from negativity, it will also help with releasing negative emotions.

BLACK TOURMALINE

◇◇◇◇◇◇

This is an amazing crystal for protection, especially psychic protection from negative entities. Black Tourmaline grounds your energy, opening up the connection between the earth and your spirit. This stone also releases deep feelings of anger and unworthiness, helping you rid yourself of negative thoughts that may be blocking you from living your life to its full potential and helping you understand yourself better in the process. It can also be used in meditation, or by carrying it with you, and sleeping with it in your pillowcase can give you a hefty dose of cleansing in your auric field that carries over into your physical body. As well as this, leaving Black Tourmaline in your home will provide protection and shield you from negative energy.

TIGER'S EYE

◇◇◇◇◇◇◇

Tiger's Eye is specifically great for protecting those planning a new venture. This is because it is known as the stone of good luck, and with good luck and determination you are then protected from failure. When I started my crystal business, Athena's Crystals, I wrote down on a piece of paper 'I will always succeed'. When I slept, I kept a piece of Tiger's Eye on this note with the intention of programming the crystal with what I had written. I would then carry it round with me during the day. When I had my Tiger's Eye crystal in my pocket, I thought up some of my best-selling products, such as the Athena Necklace, and I felt the energy of this crystal assisting me throughout my journey and protecting me as I entered this new phase in my life.

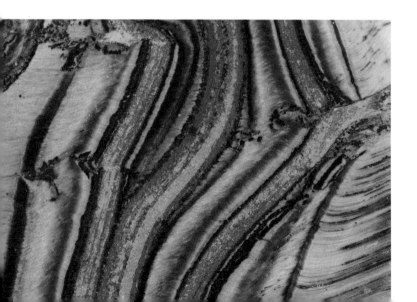

ENERGY VAMPIRES

Let's talk about something that's very common but extremely alarming . . . energy vampires! I learnt about these from Beatrice Kamau on 'The Self Love Fix' podcast and would definitely recommend checking her podcast out if you haven't already – she's amazing! As human beings all of our energies naturally become depleted when we go through a stressful time, if we are upset or if we are generally just exhausted, and we all need to regain our energy from somewhere. Obviously we provide ourselves with physical energy in the form of food and sleep, but when it comes to our emotions we need to learn how to replenish our own source of emotional energy when we are feeling depleted.

A lot of spiritual people know how to do this, whether it be through meditation, working with crystals, shadow work, etc. However, many people can't do this and they will literally feed off of other people's energy to soothe themselves. This can look like seeking external validation, putting other people down, being bitter or jealous towards others, or just generally draining people of their energy. These people are known in the spiritual community as 'energy vampires' and they will literally do this because they are unable to soothe and replenish their own energy, so they feed off the energy of people around them. Although most people won't realize they are doing this, it is still important to be aware of people around you who could be leeching off your energy.

I know this is true because I was once an energy vampire myself. When I was younger I was deeply insecure, and the only way I knew how to make myself feel better was to put others down. When my first sister was born I despised her because I thought that if I wasn't the cutest, youngest child any more then who would care about me? She also had these beautiful, bouncy curls that everyone in our family would swoon over, and this triggered me deeply because I was blessed with about three hairs on my entire head. So what did I do? Apart from sneaking into her room in the middle of the night with a pair of zig-zag scissors and cutting her hair off, I picked on her. I made her whole young life a living hell by switching at any moment from her best friend to her worst enemy. I am deeply ashamed of this behaviour now but luckily she's a lot more mature than I was at her age and understands the way I acted came from a place of jealousy. Whatever she did, I had to do better. But the truth is I wasn't in competition with her, I was in competition with myself. This same narrative presented itself to me throughout my teens in the form of gossiping, hanging out with people for social recognition and tearing apart anyone else's accomplishments. Why? Because I wasn't happy within myself. Back then I didn't know how to soothe my own emotions, I didn't have the same tools and knowledge I do now, so I fed off other people's energy to make mine feel somewhat more stable. With that being said, here are my top tips to protect yourself against energy vampires . . .

Tips for
Protection Against Energy Vampires

1

Cleanse your environment and body of negative energy regularly. You can do this with incense, Palo Santo, crystals (I'd recommend Selenite), sound cleansing – do what feels most effective for you!

2

Carry a piece of Black Tourmaline with you. For an added boost of protection I always wear a Black Tourmaline ring on my left hand. This is because it is believed that your dominant hand (the hand you write with) is associated with how you give out energy into the world, whereas your non-dominant hand (the hand you don't write with, aka my left hand) is associated with how you receive energy from the environment around you. Therefore wearing a protective crystal on my left hand will ensure I am protected from any negative energies I may receive in my day-to-day life.

3

A positive mental attitude! This may sound vague, but positivity is a sure way to ensure any negative energy thrown your way will bounce straight off you.

What/who in your life is draining
your energy?

....

....

....

....

....

....

....

What are the ways you like to soothe
your own energy?

....

....

....

....

....

....

....

PROTECTION FOR TRAVEL

Did you know that certain crystals are known to have specific qualities that can calm our nerves and keep us safe whilst travelling? You can hold a crystal in your hand and set your intention for a safe journey or successful trip and simply carry it with you to benefit from its energies. Another popular method is to incorporate a crystal into your jewellery or pop it in your bra or pocket so it is as close to you as possible. No matter how you are travelling, there is a crystal that can help you! So let's explore the best crystals for travel and all their unique properties.

Malachite

<small>◇◇◇◇◇◇◇◇</small>

It is said that Malachite has specific properties of protecting its user from danger and accidents of all kinds, making it a popular choice for safe travel. It is a great stone for assisting you with change, which can come in handy if you are suffering from jet lag or even moving abroad! It will also act as a guardian angel for you on your travels, because it is said to absorb, and therefore protect you from, negative energies.

Amethyst and Tiger's Eye

<small>◇◇◇◇◇◇◇◇</small>

Amethyst and Tiger's Eye are a must-have for the car. Amethyst is a great crystal for providing you with protection whilst driving. This is because its calming energies help relieve stress, ensuring you keep a level head when behind the wheel. Tiger's Eye is also a protective stone that has been traditionally used by travellers for many generations.

Sodalite

<small>◇◇◇◇◇◇◇◇</small>

Sodalite is arguably the best crystal to use when you are jetting off on a plane, as it is a highly protective stone and is said to keep you safe during air travel. If you are an anxious flyer this will be especially great for you as it is the ultimate calming crystal and brings order and calmness to the mind, making it easier to attain inner peace.

YOUR POWER

Your true power lies within your energy and how you use it. That is why it is so important to keep it protected! I don't know about you, but I can go out and have such a positive, productive day but if I return home and I feel bad energy as soon as I walk in the door, my mood shifts. Using crystals to amplify positivity in your home, your workspace and around other people will fundamentally impact your energy in the most positive way. I hope you can implement the tips and tricks in this chapter to keep harmonious energy flowing through all areas of your life and ultimately to help you step into and maintain your power!

chapter 6.

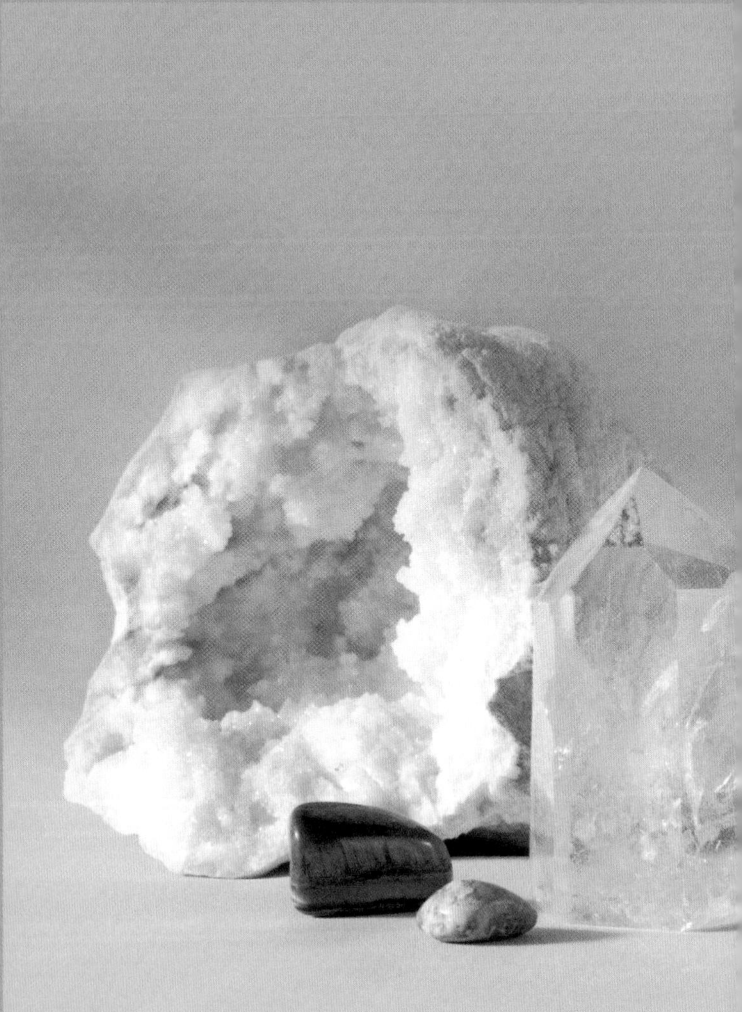

CRYSTALS FOR MANIFESTATION

CRYSTALS FOR
MANIFESTATION

You may have heard of 'the law of attraction' before and wondered what it actually means. Put simply, it is a universal law which suggests that the energy you put out into the world is the same energy you'll attract back into your life. Have you ever met someone who things just seem to work out for, who always seems to be so positive? That is a prime example of the law of attraction in action – the positive energy they are putting out they are also attracting back, giving them more reason to be positive. And the cycle just continues. With that in mind, have you ever met a person who is like a dark cloud, surrounded by negative energy? The kind of person who always assumes the worst is going to happen and, surprise surprise, it usually does? That is also the law of attraction, and that person was me for a very long time until I learnt how to manifest.

When I first started learning about manifestation I was mentally in a very dark place and was willing to give anything a go, even if I didn't fully believe in it yet. I started educating myself on the law of attraction by listening to 'The Dominating Edge' podcast by Jeff Hammer on my dog walk every morning. His podcast talks about the law of attraction and how to use it to change your life, and after a week of listening to it, it's safe to say the law of attraction became an obsession of mine. During this time I was also educating myself on specific uses of different crystals and how they can work alongside the law of attraction to amplify the positive energy you are sending out into the universe. Since then, I've combined the law of attraction and crystals to manifest everything in my life – my business, my social media following, my dream car and home – and you can too! The process of manifestation involves intentionally putting out positive intentions or thoughts of what you want to happen so that the same energy can be returned to you. Manifestation isn't some millennial phenomenon; you can find it littered throughout history. Buddha said, 'all that we are is the result of what we have thought,' and William Shakespeare wrote, 'there is nothing either good or bad, but thinking makes it so.'

If you are reading this thinking, 'I've already tried manifesting and it doesn't work for me, why does it work for others and not for me?', let me offer you a different perspective . . . First of all, your answer is in your question. Your manifestations aren't coming true because what you are putting out into the universe is that 'they're not coming true, they're not coming true', so guess what, they're not going to come true. Think of it this way, when you go to a restaurant and order your food you don't sit there and obsess over when your food is coming unless you go into the restaurant already starving. If you are not desperately hungry, you trust the process that the food is coming to you at some point and therefore you don't obsess over when it will arrive. The same applies with the law of attraction. If you are so desperate for whatever it is you are manifesting to come true then you are going to be thinking from that 'starving' position, from a place of lack. As soon as you start fuelling that manifestation from a place of lack, whatever it is you desire won't materialize because all you are seeing is it not coming true and that is the message you are sending out to the universe.

Contrary to some videos you may see on TikTok, manifestation is a daily practice. We are manifesting 24/7 whether we like it or not, and no, that does not mean every bad thought we have is going to materialize into our reality. It is the constant repetition of thoughts and beliefs in our subconscious mind that will materialize into our reality. But the most important thing is that you have to believe that it works. If you are just starting out on your manifestation journey this can be really difficult. When I first heard about the law of attraction I honestly thought someone was pulling my leg. But after learning more about it and then implementing the practice of manifestation into my daily life, I can now say I am a firm believer in the law of attraction. Further along my journey, I was drawn to astrology, the signs of the zodiac, the cycles of the moon and how they affect the process of manifestation. What I learnt transformed the way I manifest and how quickly I saw results. However, the real game-changer was when I started combining manifesting with crystals – it completely transformed my life! In this chapter I will share with you how I manifest, how you can combine your unique astrology to boost your manifestations and which crystals I use to amplify my practices so that you can also become a master manifester!

GET INTENTIONAL WITH
YOUR DESIRES

Let's talk about the most important thing you need to do to effectively manifest. If you haven't already, you need to get intentional with your desires. You need to ask yourself, 'what do I actually want?' You may already have a rough idea, but you need to be SPECIFIC with what it is you actually want to manifest. If you want a new home, what exactly does that home look like? Where would it be? If you want to increase your following on social media, how many followers do you want? What kind of content would you like to create? This is because it's not about what you want, it's about how what you want makes you feel. To attract what you want to manifest you need to be on the same frequency as the version of you that already has that thing. It is also important to think about how you will feel once you have what you desire in your life, rather than just the material thing itself. Focusing on how you want to feel emotionally is crucial to becoming the best manifester you can be. For example, when I was manifesting 1 million followers on TikTok, I wasn't just focusing on wanting those 1 million followers. I was focusing on the fact that I wanted to create a platform of like-minded people who were in a similar position to me and wanted to change their lives. I wanted to offer advice and help people because that is what brings me emotional fulfilment. As soon as I started fuelling this manifestation from a place of emotional fulfilment rather than just stats on a screen, that is when I really started noticing drastic results. I started my TikTok account in May 2021 and by the end of 2021 I had 300,000 followers, due to manifestation and a lot of hard work. However, I began to become obsessed over the stats and follower count which left me feeling defeated and uninspired. This had a knock-on effect and my following stopped growing for a while, until I changed my perspective. I remembered why I created my account in the first place and focused on the emotional side, and this changed everything. Within seven months my following grew to nearly a million and I felt more inspired than ever before, because I was focusing on my emotions!

What are the three biggest things you would like to manifest?

1. ....
   ....

2. ....
   ....

3. ....
   ....

How would manifesting these things make you feel?

1. ....
   ....
   ....

2. ....
   ....
   ....

3. ....
   ....

NEW MOON MAGIC

A new moon happens once a month when the moon and the sun conjoin in the sky. This moon represents new, fresh beginnings, and serves as the perfect time to reflect on the previous thirty days, which we call the past lunar cycle. As I mentioned earlier, manifestation is an everyday practice. However, new moons are a very powerful time to manifest your desires, set intentions and make any fresh starts in your life. Since the moon is renewing itself, it is the perfect time to renew yourself too! The new moon symbolizes a new cycle, an energy of new beginnings where you plant seeds and ask for what you want in life. So let me share with you my absolute favourite new-moon manifestation ritual.

The Diary Entry Method

For this method you are literally going to pretend you are ten years old again, you've just got home from school, you crack out that diary and you are going to write about your day (I even like to start by writing 'Dear Diary' at the top of the page). Before you start writing your diary entry, date the paper the exact date you are writing it on but in one year's time. For example, if you are using the diary method on 8 August 2023, then you will want to date the top of your paper '8 August 2024'. Next, ask yourself the question 'where do I want to be in a year?' Now this is going to look different to everyone, so spend a few moments visualizing what your dream life will look like in a year's time. Where will you be living? Are you in a relationship?

What does your career look like? But more importantly, what does your day-to-day life look like? Once you have a clear idea of what your dream life looks like in a year's time, it's time to start writing your diary entry. Write it as if you are literally documenting a normal day in this dream life exactly one year from now, and make sure you write it in the present tense. What I love about this technique is that it forces you to be specific; you have to think about exactly what it is you want and what it will look like and feel like in your day-to-day life. You can write for as long as you like – just do what feels right to you. I normally write a page or two. After writing this diary entry, I like to fold it up and keep it in a safe place with crystals that have specific properties related to manifestation to really amplify the energy of my manifestation! So with that being said, let me share with you my favourite crystals to help amplify my manifestations . . .

Clear Quartz

◇◇◇◇◇◇◇◇

Any time I am actively trying to manifest a desire I will always grab my Clear Quartz. This is because Clear Quartz is the most powerful energy amplifying stone on the planet, giving the positive energy I am sending out into the universe an added boost! Also, if you pair this with any other crystal it will also amplify the energy of that crystal. What this means is that if you have a crystal that is known for attracting love, such as Rose Quartz, pairing it with Clear Quartz will make the properties of Rose Quartz even more powerful! Quartz is said to absorb energy from sunlight and the life force in plants, trees and flowers which it will store and concentrate so this energy can be released. The energy that Clear Quartz stores has been used for centuries by many spiritual healers for both physical and emotional healing work, or even magic. This crystal can also help you gain clarity about what you want and is believed to raise your vibration to match your desires, making it a lot easier to manifest!

Tiger's Eye

◇◇◇◇◇◇◇

It's no surprise that one of my favourite crystals for manifesting is Tiger's Eye, since it's literally known as 'the good luck stone'. This crystal also supports necessary change in all aspects of your life, allowing you to manifest at the highest level. If you want assistance finding your inner roar, allow Tiger's Eye to give you courage and the strength of a tiger to demand all of your desires.

Labradorite

◇◇◇◇◇◇◇

My favourite crystal of all time. This gorgeous iridescent gemstone that glows in rainbow metallic colours is not only beautiful; it is also powerful. Known as 'the stone of magic', it is amazing for self-discovery and awakening your awareness of your inner spirit and psychic abilities – bringing your magical powers to the surface. This will allow you to look inward and use your inner magic to be the best manifester you can be!

Howlite

◇◇◇◇◇◇◇

This gorgeous white and grey stone is great for manifestation because it allows us to be open and effectively visualize our deepest desires, therefore calling them into our reality. Howlite is a crystal that encourages patience in those who use it, and a key part of manifestation is patience. After asking the universe for what it is we want to manifest, we need patience to trust that our desires have been heard! This calming stone is the perfect ally for those who want to manifest but struggle with waiting for their manifestations to come true.

Leopard Skin Jasper

◇◇◇◇◇◇◇

Welcome this crystal into your life like an old friend. It is the ultimate stone to keep near you during stressful times and ease your emotions, making you stronger in body, heart, mind and spirit! It will bring a sense of peace, serenity and reassurance that everything will work out in your favour. When aligned with the vibration of this stone, you will be able to attract the positive vibrations that correspond to your desires, putting you in the right place at the right time, and surrounded by people who will be instrumental to your personal growth. Leopard Skin Jasper is also exceptional at attracting more luck and prosperity into your life.

CRYSTAL SHAPES

Crystals come in many different shapes and sizes. All crystals will work wonderfully at assisting you on your manifestation journey no matter what shape they are. However, some crystal shapes are known to be especially helpful when it specifically comes to manifesting.

Crystal Points

Crystal points are normally naturally occurring and are especially good for manifesting as you can focus and direct their energy with their pointed shape. For example, I always have a crystal point focused at me whilst I'm manifesting so I can really concentrate its energies on boosting my manifestation practice.

Crystal Towers

Crystal towers are very similar to points; however, they are normally larger and can stand up on their own. Again, their pointed shape is great specifically for focusing and directing the energy of that crystal, which can help enhance meditation and manifestation practices.

Crystal Pyramids

Crystal pyramids are known to be particularly helpful for manifesting because their pyramid shape is said to help connect you to a higher consciousness.

MANIFESTING WITH
YOUR ELEMENT

Combining astrology with how I use crystals has been game-changing for me on my personal manifestation journey. If you are not familiar with astrology or zodiac signs, let me briefly walk you through it. Astrology is the study of the influence that stars and planets have on human lives and the influence they can have on an individual's personality based on their zodiac sign. Your zodiac sign is determined by the position of the sun at the time of your birth and every zodiac sign is associated with a particular element – air, fire, earth or water. Therefore, when I do any of the manifestation practices mentioned in this chapter with crystals I always like to incorporate the element of my zodiac sign. For me, I find this personalizes my manifestation rituals and makes me feel way more connected to whichever ritual I am doing at that time, resulting in the process being far more powerful. So, with that being said, let me share with you the crystal manifestation ritual I'd recommend for you based on the element associated with your zodiac sign.

My element is . . .

....

....

....

Air Signs *(Gemini, Libra and Aquarius)*

Air signs are known for being the communicators of the zodiac. They are often very sociable characters, perceptive and sometimes a bit flighty. If you are an air sign, you can incorporate smoke or other air element practices to amplify your manifestations.

Manifestation Ritual for the Air Signs

◇ Pick a crystal that aligns with what you are wanting to manifest or any crystal you feel intuitively drawn to.

◇ Cleanse your energy with some incense by passing the smoke gently over each and every part of your body.

◇ Take some deep breaths until you feel like you are in a relaxed state.

◇ Tell the crystal what you would like to manifest (if you've never done this before you might feel embarrassed, but just roll with it).

◇ Close your ritual by thanking the crystal for the energy it will help attract into your life.

Earth Signs (*Taurus, Virgo and Capricorn*)

Earth signs are given a bad reputation for being 'their way or the highway' kind of people, but this is because they value feeling secure and grounded. They enjoy the pleasures of life and are known for being perfectionists. However, earth signs are known for being some of the most reliable people you can meet and they make wonderful friends! If you are an earth sign, you can massively benefit from the use of the element of earth to amplify your manifestations.

Manifestation Ritual for the Earth Signs

◇ First decide what you are wanting to manifest and pick a crystal that has properties that support that manifestation.

◇ Get out in nature! Step out into your garden, a nearby park or forest, just wherever you feel most connected to nature.

◇ Lie on your back, take a few cleansing breaths and quiet your mind.

◇ Hold the crystal in your hand and visualize its energy radiating into your body and providing you with the energy you need to achieve your manifestation.

◇ Continue this until you feel called to stop.

◇ Finally, take a deep cleansing breath and express gratitude, either internally or out loud, for the work that was done.

Fire Signs *(Aries, Leo and Sagittarius)*

Fire signs are known for being, shock horror, the most hot-headed of the zodiac signs. However, their passionate energy also has its positives, such as being enthusiastic and warm individuals who enjoy uplifting others. If you are a fire sign, you can use the element of fire to amplify your manifestations.

Manifestation Ritual for the Fire Signs

◇ Place a candle in a setting where you feel safe and comfortable, and will not be disturbed!

◇ Place a crystal that aligns with what you are wanting to manifest or any crystal you feel intuitively drawn to in front of your candle.

◇ Close your eyes and visualize the situation you would like to see manifested as if it is already happening.

◇ Now take a pen and paper and write down your manifestation and place it under the unlit candle.

◇ Finally, light the candle, setting the intention that working with this fire element and crystal will attract your manifestation into your reality.

◇ Close the ritual with some words of gratitude for the crystal and fire granting your wish!

Water Signs *(Cancer, Scorpio and Pisces)*

Water signs are known for being the most emotional signs of the zodiac, and as a Scorpio, I can confirm that is the case. They have extremely deep emotions and can sometimes feel overwhelmed by their own feelings. That being said, they are also known as the most naturally intuitive of the zodiac signs, meaning they are natural-born manifesters. So, as a water sign myself, here is my favourite manifestation practice that connects me with both my element and my love of crystals.

Manifestation Ritual for the Water Signs

◇ Get a cup and fill it with water (the type of cup or glass really isn't important).

◇ Hold the cup of water up to your chest.

◇ Close your eyes and visualize whatever it is you are trying to manifest coming true in your life and what that would look and feel like to you. Do this for as long as you like!

◇ When you feel called to stop, open your eyes and pick up a crystal that is known to amplify energy, such as Clear Quartz, and say aloud to the crystal, 'I am now open to receive these blessings and am so grateful to this crystal for delivering all of my desires.'

◇ Then simply drink the water, as it is now charged with your intentions. I know this is going to sound a little bizarre but for over twenty years, Dr Masaru Emoto studied and provided scientific evidence of how the molecular structure of water transforms when it is exposed to human words, sounds, thoughts and even intentions! He writes all about his findings in his 2004 *New York Times* bestseller, *The Hidden Messages in Water*.

 Finally, take the crystal you used in this ritual and carry it with you for the next few weeks and let it work its magic!

YOUR MOON SIGN AND CRYSTALS

Did you know there is far more to astrology than just your zodiac sign? Your zodiac sign, also known as your sun sign, is only one component of your 'birth chart'. If you are sitting there scratching your head on what a birth chart even means, allow me to explain. Your birth chart is a precise snapshot of the position of all of the planets at the exact moment you were born. You can find out your birth chart online – my favourite website for this is alabe.com. Broadly speaking, the position of each planet in your birth chart represents a different type of energy and how that energy will affect your personality in different areas of your life.

Your Moon Sign and your Manifestation Journey

In our birth chart, the zodiac sign the moon is in on your chart is very important. In astrology, the moon is known to rule our emotions. As I have touched on in this chapter, the key to being a master manifester is focusing on how achieving that manifestation would make you feel rather than the actual manifestation itself. Low-vibrational emotions such as shame, guilt and sadness will attract more of that into your life. The same goes for high-vibrational emotions such as happiness and excitement, so putting positive emotions behind your manifestations will bring them to you so much faster and more effectively. Therefore, understanding your moon sign will really help you understand your emotions. When we are in tune with our emotions we can more effectively focus on positive emotions and, as a result, be better manifesters. Can we control our emotions? No. But we can make space for them, separate ourselves from them and become aware that we are not the emotion itself; we are simply the human experiencing that emotion.

As I mentioned earlier, when we experience a negative emotion it will attract more of that into our lives. A crucial turning point in manifesting is learning to turn these negative feelings into an opportunity to understand yourself more deeply and say, 'Okay, great, this is a good indicator of what I do not want to feel and now I have a clearer understanding of what it is I actually do want to manifest.' We are all different and events will affect our emotions differently. For example, if you have a water sign moon like me you are more likely to feel emotion on a deeper level than others. As I've said before, whenever I've been through an emotionally heavy time, such as a break-up, I let it destroy me for a while. Whereas now I can acknowledge that and say, 'You know what, it's really important for me to feel safe and valued in my relationships, so that is what I am going to manifest going forward.' A way in which I became more deeply connected with my moon sign is through crystals. Did you know that every crystal is associated with a specific zodiac sign? Therefore, working with crystals that are specifically associated with your moon sign will help you become more in tune with your emotions and allow you to use positive emotions to fuel your manifestations. These are the crystals I would recommend for you based on your moon sign:

Aries Moon

For you crazy beauties I recommend Red Jasper, because this stone helps you tackle problems without being aggressive, which is a trait Aries moons are known to struggle with! It will also help you keep focused and motivated because you guys work hard! This stone is also very helpful for those who overwork themselves and spread themselves too thin which can lead to burnout, which Aries moons tend to do. It is also amazing at increasing sexual passion between lovers, not that you guys need help in that department, but come on, you're an Aries moon and you can never have enough spice, right? It will also help protect you from bad luck and accidents and if you've ever met someone with an Aries moon you will know they are probably among the clumsiest people you've ever met. Red Jasper is also an amazing stone for helping you think before you act, and Aries moons are arguably the most hot-headed sign of the entire zodiac.

Taurus Moon

If you have a Taurus moon I would definitely recommend getting your hands on some Rose Quartz. Tauruses are known for being the healers of the zodiac but Rose Quartz is the healer of the heart. Taurus moons are also known to value feeling comfortable and safe, which makes Rose Quartz perfect for you as it's a highly protective stone that promotes peace and harmony in your life. Taurus moons generally make great romantic partners and Rose Quartz is often used to attract a romantic partner if you are single or to deepen a connection in an existing relationship.

 ## Gemini Moon

For the social queen of the zodiac I recommend nothing less than Citrine. Citrine is actually classed as a birthstone for Gemini. A birthstone is a gemstone that represents a person's period of birth, usually the month or zodiac sign, meaning working with its energies will be especially powerful for you. Gemini moons are always bringing happy, positive energy. You will literally light up any room you are in, and Citrine will amplify your own feelings of happiness and positivity and encourage you to continue shining your light into the world! Gemini moons love to see all the possibilities of life and really think outside of the box, which makes Citrine perfect for you as it also inspires creativity and imagination. As well as this, it also sustains the process of transforming your dreams into tangible form, making it an excellent stone for manifestation!

Cancer Moon

If you have a Cancer moon, I immediately love you and want to be your best friend. You guys are just the cutest and I think every Cancer moon needs White Rainbow Moonstone in their life. As a Cancer moon myself, you don't need me to tell you that you guys truly feel ALL the feels. Meaning you feel your emotions on such a deep level it can sometimes even scare you. This is why White Rainbow Moonstone is great for you since it is known for amplifying feelings of hope and positivity whilst also attracting harmony and balance into your life. Cancer moons are amazing at being empathetic and understanding towards others, but this crystal will help you step into your own power and gain inner confidence.

Leo Moon

For you spotlight-loving Leo moons I would recommend Tiger's Eye. This crystal will be perfect for you as it inspires creativity and will help you utilize your talents and abilities so you can continue thriving in the 'main character' energy that you guys naturally radiate. Leo moons are known for being super proud, supportive and protective of their friends, but Tiger's Eye is a crystal with protective properties so that you can also be protected! Tiger's Eye is also known to attract wealth and the judgement needed to maintain that wealth, which will be particularly helpful for the Leo moons out there with a bit of a shopping addiction. What can I say, you guys like the finer things in life and I love that about you! This crystal will also help you manifest at your highest level, attracting happiness, health and fulfilment into your life, and continue being the fabulous queen that you are!

Virgo Moon

If you are a Virgo moon, you are the boss. Virgo moons are known for being detail orientated, verging on obsessively anal, but that is your charm. Amazonite is the perfect crystal for a Virgo moon because it is known for its soothing properties, meaning you can continue being your perfectionist self but also keep your stress levels down whilst doing so. Virgo moons will show you they care by always being willing to give a helping hand and Amazonite will be great for you because it fills the heart with determination to do good in the world.

Libra Moon

There are no words to describe how much I love Libra moons and for these beautiful individuals I would recommend beautiful Lapis Lazuli. If you are a Libra moon, I'm sure you are always there to listen to your friends' worries. Lapis Lazuli is an amazing stone for encouraging you to stick to your principles and rise above pettiness, ensuring you don't get too caught up in others' issues or get involved with any negative gossip! Libra moons are so fun to be around and whilst being great conversationalists, they are also great peacekeepers. Lapis Lazuli will align with your energy beautifully by helping you maintain your integrity and have trusting, positive relationships with those around you.

 ## Scorpio Moon

The energy that a Scorpio moon gives off is truly mesmerizing and magnetic. Scorpios are known for being the zodiac sign of death and rebirth. With that in mind, I believe every Scorpio moon needs some Malachite in their life. Known as 'the stone of transformation', Malachite will assist a Scorpio moon on their journey of constant growth. A Scorpio moon has the biggest heart and will do anything for you, once you earn their trust. My best friend is a Scorpio moon and she will always be the first person I call when I have done something really stupid and don't know who to turn to and she will be there in a flash, no questions asked. Because this moon sign has such a big heart, they can often take on the burden of everyone else's issues and put their own needs to one side. Malachite will really benefit a Scorpio moon as it is also referred to as 'the stone of protection'. It is said to absorb negative energies and pollutants from the atmosphere and from the body, making sure Scorpio moons are looking after themselves as well as everyone else.

Sagittarius Moon

If you are a Sagittarius moon, you are pure fire, in the best way. You can always rely on Sagittarius moons to be the life and soul of the party or to speak up for themselves if they are being disrespected. So if this is you, I would recommend Sodalite, as it is the ultimate calming crystal and is ideal for those who are particularly defensive or impulsive (Sagittarius moons are known for being a tad hot-headed in arguments). Sodalite will help a Sagittarius moon shift their mindset from emotional to rational, rather than acting on impulse and perhaps saying something they don't really mean.

Capricorn Moon

If you are a Capricorn moon, you hold the 'big dick' energy of the zodiac. This means you are a natural-born provider, you have no problem getting shit done and you are normally very career driven. Vasonite would be a great crystal for you as it is a powerful crystal with a high vibration that will assist you in following your true heart's desire, allowing you to continue to embody that go-getter energy! Capricorn moons are very inspirational people but sometimes they are known to struggle with forming deep, meaningful connections with others. Again, this will make Vasonite a great crystal for this moon sign as it is known for encouraging love and companionship in life.

Aquarius Moon

There is a special place in my heart for an Aquarius moon, as my two younger sisters are Aquarius moons! If you have this moon sign, you are so wonderfully weird and unique, you march to your own drum and do so with pride. You are the best people to party with because you don't care about what other people think and you dance like nobody is watching. Being a natural performer also runs the risk of neglecting your own needs in order to uplift others. So if you are an Aquarius moon I would recommend Amethyst, which encourages individuals to give themselves the love they need to allow their energy to flow again, meaning you can continue showing up as the entertainer you were born to be!

Pisces Moon

Pisces moons are known as the dreamers of the zodiac. Whether it is a vintage record collection or an abstract artwork, Pisces individuals find beauty in everything around them. Pisces moons are usually the designated therapist of their friendship group; they are always there to listen and offer advice to a friend in need. Pisces feel everything on a deep level, which is why Clear Quartz is the crystal for them. It is known to absorb negativity and transform it into rays of healing, and since Pisces are sensitive to the emotions of others, this crystal will help them care for their own needs.

Manifestation
Journal

I want to share with you one of my most crucial turning points and fundamental basics in my manifestation journey – journaling. I cannot stress enough how important journaling is and how the power of pen to paper is so underestimated. So let me explain what a manifestation journal is and how you can use it. First, you need to buy a journal. This doesn't have to be anything fancy or expensive, just a plain notebook that is aesthetically pleasing to you and that you can use specifically for your manifestation journaling. Once you have got your journal, it's time to get manifesting. So let me share with you my all-time favourite manifestation journaling techniques.

Affirmation Method

◇ If you are just starting manifesting with your journal, this is the exercise I'd recommend you do first!

◇ The most important part of manifesting is becoming intentional with your desires, so the first step you'll want to do is think of what exactly it is you are trying to manifest. Perhaps start out with ten goals in mind.

◇ Once you are clear on these goals, turn them into affirmations. Write these affirmations in the present tense as if they are already true. Here are some examples:

If you are trying to manifest self-confidence you could write the affirmation 'I am beautiful inside and out, I love myself unconditionally.'

If you want to manifest new opportunities in your career you could write 'Opportunities present themselves to me constantly, I am so lucky to be thriving in my career.'

If you would like to manifest health for your friends and family (and yes, you can manifest on the behalf of others!) you could write an affirmation saying 'I am so grateful for the good health of all my friends and family.'

Write all of the affirmations that support what you are trying to manifest on the first page of your journal.
Then whenever you go to use your journal, or just want to manifest, you can simply go to the first page of your journal and read these affirmations aloud or in your head.

5x55 Method

Choose an affirmation that supports what you want to manifest, and write it in the present tense, for example, 'I am so happy I have my dream job.'

Write this affirmation fifty-five times in a row during five consecutive days.

At the end of the five days all that is left to do is let go, knowing that the universe will deliver your manifestation!

369 Method

The number three is said to align individuals with the universe, the number six symbolizes strength and nine is the number of release and healing. The combination of these numbers is said to be sacred; therefore combining them into a manifestation ritual helps you harness the power of both numerology and the law of attraction. Nikola Tesla, an engineer and scientist known for designing the alternating-current (AC) electric system, is alleged to have stated: 'If you only knew the magnificence of the 3, 6, and 9, then you would have a key to the universe.' The 369 method involves writing down affirmations that support what you want to manifest, such as 'I am wealthy', three times in the morning, six times at midday and nine times in the evening for ninety-six days.

Letter Method

◇ First of all, think of the BIGGEST thing you want to manifest, that one dream that you wish would come true. I don't care how ridiculous it may seem – remember, no dream is too big!

◇ Start a new page in your journal, this is going to be your letter.

◇ Imagine that you are writing a letter to a person you have a really strong connection with. It doesn't matter if it's your best friend, your mum, your sister, your dad, just whoever you feel really strongly connected to.

You are then going to write a letter to this person telling them how you have achieved this dream and exactly how it happened, for example, 'Dear Mum, I am so excited and just had to send you a letter to tell you! Can't believe I just got offered my dream role in my favourite TV show! This is how it happened …'

Write the letter the way you'd normally converse with this person and really try to capture the feeling of excitement and live the experience exactly how you would if this was a real letter and your dream had come true.

After writing this letter, simply sign the letter off with your name and close the journal knowing you have sent that manifestation out to the universe!

Using Crystals with your Journal

I always use crystals to amplify the power of these journaling methods. I keep certain crystals that are known to amplify energy or attract good luck, such as Clear Quartz and Tiger's Eye, on top of my journal whenever I'm not using it so that the crystals can be charged with the intentions of whatever it is I am trying to manifest.

Another technique I love for combining crystals with journaling is using a crystal pen! I always use my Clear Quartz crystal pen from Etsy when writing down my manifestations to amplify the energy further!

MANIFESTATION METHODS

If journaling isn't your thing, there are plenty of other manifestation methods that don't involve writing that are super effective! I personally find that combining journaling with alternative methods is the most powerful for me, so if you are new to manifesting I'd recommend giving all of the methods a try and seeing what feels right for you! This is your journey and manifestation should never feel like a chore or homework, it should be something you enjoy. At the beginning of my journey I forced myself to do all of these methods because I thought it would provide me with the best results. I was sorely mistaken. The whole point of manifesting is that the energy you are putting out is returned to you; therefore, when you are actively trying to manifest you should always be in a happy, positive frame of mind! So let's talk about my other favourite manifestation methods.

Creating a Vision Board

Vision Board for Short-Term Goals

This is the vision board I suggest you make for everything you want to manifest in the near future. This is your chance to be specific. Do you want to manifest a specific amount of money? A specific job? A specific holiday? When you are clear on what it is you want to manifest, find some photos on the internet that represent these goals. For example, when I was manifesting a holiday to Italy I would find photos of the hotel I wanted to stay in. You can just use Google Images for this but I love using the Pinterest app so the photos are all aesthetically pleasing. Once you are happy with all the pictures you want for your vision board then edit them all together into a collage (I use the app PicCollage for this!). When you have your finished collage, set that collage as the lock-screen image on your phone and laptop. The reason this is beneficial is because you will then have to look at these images every time you use your devices, keeping your manifestations fresh in your mind.

Vision Board for Long-Term Goals

This vision board is going to be physical rather than digital and is a great method for manifesting any long-term goals you may have. You go through the same process, finding pictures online that align with what you want to manifest long term. These manifestations are a lot more general compared to the short-term vision board. For example, on my physical vision board I have photos of what I want my ideal home to look like, my dream wedding dress, my dream car and photos of all the countries I want to visit. I would also recommend adding any positive quotes that inspire you as well as photos of things that put you in a good mood so that you are in a positive frame of mind whilst looking at your vision board. Once you have your pictures, print them off and glue them on to a piece of canvas or card. I would recommend hanging this vision board somewhere you see it often – my physical vision board is hung by the mirror in my bathroom so I can always look at it when I'm brushing my teeth and doing my skincare routine! On top of my physical vision board I like to place Clear Quartz to amplify the energy of my manifestations. From personal experience this works like a charm and half of the dream pictures that are on my vision board have already come true!

Visualization

Neurology studies suggest visualization can help bring about better futures for those that practise it; some studies even suggest that it can change the brain! A 2018 brain imaging study led by researchers at the University of Colorado Boulder and the Icahn School of Medicine at Mount Sinai shows that imagining a threat lights up similar regions as experiencing it does, making manifestation a very powerful technique.

Visualization is a practice that simply involves closing your eyes and imagining a certain scenario. For example, if you are manifesting your dream job, simply close your eyes and imagine what it would be like working at this dream job. When I was manifesting my dream car I would set a timer on my phone for a couple of minutes and just sit, close my eyes and imagine I was driving this car around. I would try and feel all the sensations of putting the roof down, driving down windy country roads with the music on full blast. I'll tell you more about how manifesting my dream car played out in the next chapter! This technique is great because it mimics your body experiencing the emotion that it would if this was your reality, and as I've said over and over again, when it comes to manifesting it is the emotion behind what you are trying to manifest which is the most powerful thing.

You can easily amplify this visualization by holding a crystal that aligns with what you are wanting to manifest. For example, if you are visualizing your dream relationship, hold a piece of Rose Quartz because of its love-attracting properties! If you are manifesting getting good results in an exam, hold a piece of Tiger's Eye for its good luck benefits! Whatever it is you are trying to manifest, there's a crystal for it.

Crystal
Manifestation
Bags

◇ Get a small bag – I love to use organza bags!

◇ Take a piece of paper and write down your manifestation. This can be multiple manifestations or just one. I normally put something along the lines of 'I'm so happy and grateful now that I have . . .' I usually do this on a new moon because I like working with the moon cycles to amplify my manifestation rituals as much as possible, but you can do this whenever you please!

◇ When you have finished writing, fold the piece of paper towards you (this is meant to symbolize drawing that energy towards you).

◇ Pick a crystal or a few crystals whose properties relate to your manifestation.

◇ Pop the paper and crystals in the bag and seal it shut.

◇ Sleep with it under your pillow until the next full moon. As I mentioned at the beginning of this chapter, crystals have been so important to all that I've manifested in my life. I even used them to manifest my own crystal business! When I was at my lowest and started educating myself on the power of crystals and manifestation, I started out with one clear vision. All I wanted to manifest was a purpose in life, to discover my full potential and what I felt I was put on this earth to do. This was when I was drawn to a beautiful Clear Quartz necklace I had bought in a South African market and had completely forgotten about. I held the necklace in my hand and set it with one simple intention which was 'I will find my purpose.' I wore this necklace constantly for the next few weeks, even in the shower. One day when I was showering, I suddenly had a vision of starting a crystal business and I knew instantly that was my purpose. I still believe to this day that setting that particular intention with that Clear Quartz necklace was the start of putting me on the path of my soul's purpose. My point is, even if you feel completely lost and have no idea what you want to do in your life, that's absolutely fine! Everyone finds their purpose at different times and everybody's journey is unique, and I hope with what you have learnt in this chapter you can start the process of manifesting everything you desire from life, whatever that may be!

My manifesting bucket list . . .

1. ....

2. ....

3. ....

4. ....

chapter 7

CRYSTALS FOR HAPPINESS

CRYSTALS FOR HAPPINESS

How do we define happiness? Is it in those fleeting moments of unexpected joy that catch us off guard? Is it in the memories made with the ones we love? Is it in our favourite meal or our favourite song? The truth is there is happiness to be found in everything, but whether we choose to see it is a different matter. Put simply, happiness is an emotion that we experience. However, how often we experience this emotion is ultimately down to us and our perception. This is a tough pill to swallow but the truth is we are all in control of our own happiness. No matter what misfortune we have experienced in our lifetime, we can decide to view things in a positive light.

Another important thing to remember about happiness is that for it to exist in your future, it has to exist in your present. What I mean by this is happiness is not rooted in achieving your next goal, and if you live your life this way then the feeling of happiness will be something you are always grasping at rather than something that's attainable. This is summed up perfectly by entrepreneur and podcast host Steven Bartlett who wrote, 'By the way, if you're not happy now, there's no sports car, amount of followers, bust size, promotion, social media feedback or material possession that's going to fundamentally change that. External validation isn't happiness, it's a hamster wheel. Happiness is an inside job.'

I was introduced to Steven Bartlett's podcast, 'Diary of a CEO', by a friend in 2021. At the time this friend had been through a rough break-up and had a real dedication to becoming the best and happiest version of themselves. They spun this difficult time in their life into an opportunity for self-development and I was always so inspired by their 'glass-half-full' outlook on life and how easily they could paint a smile across their face without it being fake. After seeing the 'Diary of a CEO' podcast live in London together, we both left obsessed with the concept of mindset and how having a positive perspective on life really does determine what you are capable of achieving and how content you will feel. It has been an honour to watch this friend achieve so much in such a short time and it's very clear that there is one reason for it – dedication. If you are not used to looking on the bright side, and trust me, for a long time I wasn't, choosing to be a positive, upbeat person does not happen overnight. You have to show up for yourself every single day, even when you don't feel like it, and try to see the good in every situation.

The hardest pill for me to swallow on my personal journey was how much I was playing a part in my own suffering. I didn't just think negatively about myself and my life, I would even pick apart a positive situation until it was negative. I was diagnosed with depression and anxiety in my late teens and was prescribed a multitude of pills to help with these issues, but I knew that wasn't going to cut it. Don't get me wrong, those with mental health conditions should always seek help from medical professionals and I'm so glad I did, but for me personally the medication was a short-term fix. I've struggled with various mental health issues for as long as I can remember and have been in some incredibly dark places where I couldn't always see a way out. This is what really got me into crystals, spirituality and my fascination with the power your mindset can have. Changing the way you think really does change the way you live.

I look back on the person I was a few years ago and I don't recognize her. I definitely wouldn't have believed you if you told me back then I would make it to where I am now. Happiness within yourself and the life you already have is the key to stepping into your power and accessing your true potential. In this chapter we will look at the daily practices that played the biggest role in contributing to my overall happiness as well as how I used crystals to transform myself from a 'glass-half-empty' to a 'glass-half-full' kind of girl.

FEEL YOUR FEELINGS

If there was one piece of advice I could give my younger self, it would be to stop 'playing' hard to get. I don't want this to be confused with not knowing your worth, but let's talk about the difference between 'playing' hard to get and 'being' hard to get. In a lot of cases, when you are playing hard to get, it's because you are doing so in the hope that the person you are talking to will then like you more. This narrative of being hot and cold with someone to keep them interested in you is a concept I see pushed a lot on social media, and is a concept I used myself. This has been a massive, and actually very recent, lesson I've had to learn the hard way. I never used to believe that my personality, and just my general sense of being, was enough to make people want me, so I thought being hot and cold with people, or 'playing' hard to get, was going to keep their attention longer. Let me be clear, this does work . . . but with the wrong people. When I say the 'wrong people' I mean the type of people whose intentions are not true, or simply people who are wrong for you in terms of compatibility.

If you genuinely love and care about someone, just tell them. If you are honest with your feelings and that scares them off, they weren't the one for you anyway. Life is far too short to not be honest with your feelings, and there is a big difference between 'being' hard to get and 'playing' hard to get. You should be hard to get, because you should know your worth and that anyone would be lucky to be a part of your life, and not everyone deserves access to your energy. But don't 'play' hard to get because of your personal insecurity, because speaking from experience, it never ends well. At heart I am the soppiest person alive; I used to give love so freely and without fear. That was until, of course, I was hurt a few times along the way. From the age of thirteen until my twenties, I was in an extremely turbulent and, for the most part, emotionally abusive relationship. The level at which this relationship affected me was so deeply embedded in my subconscious that I wasn't even aware of it. After it ended, I adopted a shield of armour in the form of an emotional wall between me and other people. But let me tell you something I learnt by doing this: not letting people connect with you on an emotional level will ultimately never lead to a happy ending.

Although I talk a lot about independence and self-sufficiency in this book, it is important to acknowledge that we humans are social beings. The relationships we share in this lifetime, whether romantic or platonic, inevitably shape who we are as individuals. And just like everything else we manifest into our lives, our vibe attracts our tribe. Surrounding yourself with positive, uplifting people is so pivotal for your personal growth and development. Having a network of people around you who inspire you and encourage you to be the best version of yourself is a beautiful thing, so please don't push them away because, like me, you were too scared of letting people get 'too close' to you. If you do have people in your life that you are grateful for, tell them that you love them. Steven Bartlett also spoke about this during the 'Diary of a CEO' live show, and he said something I didn't really understand until now, but it perfectly depicts how I felt when I was trying to fight my own feelings. He said, 'I find it hard to love, I've tried a lot, I know that this is true. So isn't it amazing, despite the odds, that I fell in love with you.' The reason I loved this quote so much is it speaks to the insecure part of us, the part that has gone through a lot of pain but is learning how to love ourselves, and others, again. So if you find it difficult to form deep connections with others without fear of being hurt, here are some crystals that can help you.

Smoky Quartz

∞∞∞∞∞

This is my go-to crystal for leaving past situations that hurt you where they belong, in the past. The properties of this crystal are great for healing from painful experiences and moving forward in a more positive way.

Amazonite

∞∞∞∞∞

As I've mentioned before, Amazonite works with the Heart Chakra (the chakra responsible for being open to receiving and giving love). As well as this, it works with the Throat Chakra, meaning you will not only be open to receiving love but you will also be able to clearly express how you want to be loved.

Blue Lace Agate

∞∞∞∞∞

This is a powerful crystal that promotes positive communication within relationships. Its calming energy will help provide emotional balance and clear your mind of negative thoughts. Blue Lace Agate also promotes forgiveness and personal growth, making it ideal for those who are struggling to move on from past hurt.

Are there any feelings you are trying
to push down?

....
....
....
....
....
....
....
....
....
....
....
....
....
....

Raising Your Vibration

If you haven't heard this term before, allow me to explain. As I mentioned in the previous chapter, to successfully manifest we must be in a positive frame of mind as the energy we put out into the universe is the energy that is returned to us. Raising your vibration is the process of purposely doing things that make you feel good so that you can manifest at the highest level and generally just feel happy! Here are my favourite ways to raise my vibration and pull me out of a demotivated slump.

Get out in Nature

If all else is failing, a sure way to raise your vibration is by taking a walk in nature. When we take time to reconnect with the natural world we are reconnecting with our roots. After all, crystals come from the earth and it is evident to me the power they hold! You can also try out a walking meditation, which I spoke about in chapter three, and take your crystals with you. Let the power of the earth lift your spirits.

Dance to your Favourite Music

Music is a powerful thing. Researchers from Western Sydney University's MARCS Institute for Brain, Behaviour and Development have even found that music increases memory and retention as well as maximizing our learning capabilities! Music can also trigger different parts of the brain that are responsible for particular emotions, memories and thoughts. Therefore listening to positive, upbeat songs often leads to a dopamine rush which in turn has a positive effect on our mental health and feelings of happiness! Also, moving your body will get the blood pumping and encourage you to tackle whatever tasks you have ahead! For more information, see: https://www.bdc.nsw.edu.au/news/lift-your-mood-with-music.

Listen to High-Frequency Music

Shanna Lee, who works as a life coach in California, states that 'frequencies' are very important to the way in which we live and that we can harness their power through the use of sound. 'We are energy at our core. We have energetic interactions going on in our bodies. And if we want to understand how to improve health, we need to understand how we're interacting with frequencies,' she says. 'There are two frequencies that the body resonates very well with, one is 432Hz and one is 444Hz, and they harmonize the patterns of our bodies. There are also certain tunings – 396, 417, 528, 639, 741, 852 – which do different things. So, 396 works a lot with the emotional plain, and with grief. 639 can affect our connections with others, and so on.' Because of this I always play high-frequency music, specifically 432Hz, in the background when I'm working (I'm playing it right now on Spotify through my speaker), and I find it really uplifts me, so give it a try! To read more, see: https://www.vice.com/en/article/eve3xz/healing-properties-music-frequencies-therapy.

Crystals

Personally, my favourite way to raise my vibration is working with crystals. What a surprise. Whether it's doing a meditation practice or simply holding them, aligning with their energies, they always put me in a good mood. If you don't know which crystals to go to for an instant mood boost, don't worry, I will reveal all later in this chapter.

HAVE A GRATITUDE ATTITUDE

Expressing gratitude has arguably been the most transformational practice along my whole journey. The universe has a funny way of giving you more of what you want when you live in a state of gratitude for what you already have. When you feel grateful for something or someone, your body automatically believes that something good is going to happen to you or has already happened to you. If you took anything from the previous chapter on manifestation it should be that what you think about you bring about. Therefore, focusing on what you are grateful for rather than what you don't have will attract more positivity into your life. I'm going to throw a lot of clichés into this chapter but every cloud does have a silver lining. They really do. What you focus on expands.

Let me give you an example. Last year I was manifesting a new car, my dream car. However, this came from a place of hating my old car. My old car was battered from my first year of not-so-responsible driving – the rear-view mirror and the glove box door had fallen off, it was basically falling apart, not to mention the odd smell that never went away after my friend left her unfinished sushi under the passenger seat. Every time I went to look at buying the new car I desired it was either too expensive or too far away. I couldn't get my head round why I wasn't able to manifest this car when I had already successfully manifested pretty much everything else in my life, and then it clicked. I wasn't going to get anywhere unless I started showing some appreciation for my beaten-up, fishy-smelling car first. I then actively started showing gratitude towards this car. I gave her a good scrub, I considered myself lucky every single time she took me where I wanted to go without breaking down, I decided to focus on what I loved about this car rather than what I hated. This went on for a couple of months until one afternoon my back tyre blew, throwing the car through a nearby bush and into a field. The bush took with it the whole front of my car along with both wing mirrors – long story short I wrote the car off. I could have seen this as an absolute disaster – all that positive thinking and for what? But I remained positive. I looked at the cloud but I focused on the silver lining; I knew deep down that the universe was removing this car for me to make room for something better. Lo and behold, a few days later I received an offer from my insurance for the price of the car which was practically enough to buy my dream car. Then a couple of days later a friend sent me a link to my dream car that was on sale less than an hour away at a great price. Don't get me wrong, I'm not saying the answer is to go and drive your car through the nearest bush. I'm saying that gratitude is your secret weapon, so use it! If you struggle with being grateful for what you already have, like I used to, here is my top practice which will make you a gratitude master . . .

Gratitude Journaling

This is a practice I do every single day. Gratitude journaling is simply writing a list of five things you are grateful for as soon as you wake up. It can be your home, a person in your life, what you have planned for the day, anything! This sets the tone of your day and really starts you off on a positive note. When I first started this, when I was in the depths of my depression, I struggled to think of two. Which when I look back now is baffling. Honestly, when you start practising gratitude every day it's like a skill that will develop and suddenly you won't be able to stop your brain from being grateful. About a week into forcing myself to do this every morning, I started thinking differently. I would walk into the bathroom and suddenly become aware of how grateful I was for my legs that were walking me there. I would turn on the shower, feel the hot water and feel like the luckiest person in the world that I had access to this hot water. Once I was making a coffee with my Nespresso machine and stood for about ten minutes, staring intently at the capsules, thinking how amazing it was that people were able to put coffee into these tiny little pods that get delivered to my door, ready for me to put into my machine to make at home. Now anyone watching may have just thought I was really high – but I was just high on life! Magic really is all around us, you just have to open your eyes.

What are five things you are currently grateful for?

1. ....
....
....

2. ....
....
....

3. ....
....
....

4. ....
....
....

5. ....
....
....
....

Crystals for Gratitude

Rose Quartz

⬦⬦⬦⬦⬦⬦⬦

This crystal is so great at encouraging us to be grateful because it helps release us from the 'lack' mentality. It replaces feelings of lack with feelings of love and compassion, allowing us to view the world through a different lens. It's the perfect crystal for those who struggle to see the good in life as it helps those who use it to reach a deeper state of appreciation.

Amethyst

⬦⬦⬦⬦⬦⬦⬦

It's unsurprising that Amethyst is a go-to gratitude crystal due to its power of calming the mind. This crystal will release any feelings of worry and stress, making it easier for us to focus on the good stuff, even when we are faced with challenges. Because this stone is known for dispelling pessimism and negativity it will work as a great tool in allowing you to be present and see more blessings wherever you go.

Clear Quartz

⬦⬦⬦⬦⬦⬦⬦

Known as 'the stone of the sun', Clear Quartz is great for encouraging optimism. It will help you maintain a positive attitude and be grateful for what you have. It is also believed that Clear Quartz connects us with the Universal Truth that we all have precisely what we need.

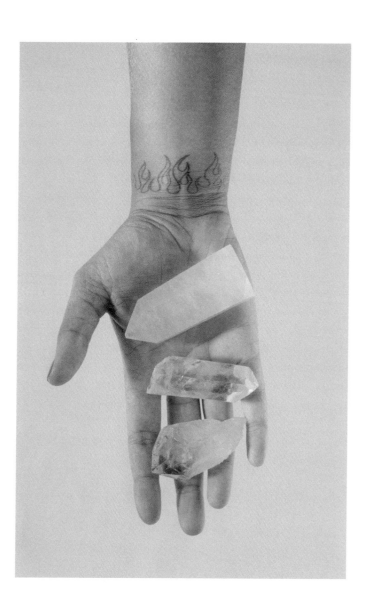

MORNING ROUTINE

You've probably heard this a million times but I cannot stress enough how important it is to have a morning routine. This is because you are far more likely to have a positive day if you start it on a positive note. A common misconception I see online is people forcing themselves into a routine that doesn't bring them joy, simply because they feel that is how they 'should' be starting their day. For example, when I first created my morning routine I would make myself get up and immediately go to the gym. Unsurprisingly, this was a routine I could not keep up for long. I am not a big fan of the gym at the best of times, especially when I am still half asleep. Your morning routine should be based on YOU as an individual, it should be something you look forward to rather than dread. If you dread your morning routine, you are missing the whole point. I'm not saying don't challenge yourself, but what I am saying is when initially starting a morning routine – make it enjoyable! This way, you are much more likely to stick to it, and you can always build on this routine and add to it further down the line.

So let me talk about my personal morning routine and how it has changed my life . . .

Create a
Morning
Routine

1. *Gratitude journaling:* As I said earlier, this just sets you off on the right foot and aligns you with the positive vibration that will attract your desires.

2. *Affirmations:* Write down three positive statements that align with what you want to manifest in your life, such as 'I have my dream job,' 'I am confident,' etc.

3. *Set an intention for the day:* What is the main thing you want to get out of this day? Do you have a specific meeting or interview you want to ace? Do you want to smash your personal target at the gym? Do you want to indulge in a self-care day and give yourself some much-needed rest? Just be clear on one main positive intention for the day ahead.

4. *Pick a crystal that aligns with that intention:* If your intention involves something where you want some luck on your side, pick up a Tiger's Eye. If you have a specific task that you need to tackle or a heavy day of work then reach for a crystal with motivation properties such as Carnelian or Red Jasper. If you are pampering yourself and having a day of relaxation then grab a calming stone such as Amethyst or Rose Quartz. This is the crystal you will want to keep with you all day, whether it's in your pocket, in your bra or on a piece of jewellery, this crystal will assist you in fulfilling your day's intention.

5. *Meditate:* Literally just spend ten minutes alone with your thoughts, letting each thought come and go whilst focusing on your breathing. I like to hold the crystal I've chosen in my hand whilst doing this to fully connect with its energies before starting my day. This short meditation will allow you to stay in touch with your inner self throughout the day knowing you can return to this state of peace at any time.

6. *Move your body:* No, this doesn't mean you have to get up and go to the gym. If that floats your boat that's great, but it certainly doesn't float mine. I personally love a good dance in front of the mirror as it helps me connect with my feminine energy and just puts me in a good mood!

> 'Set an intention
> for the day.'

FEED YOUR BRAIN GOOD STUFF

Shout out to my girl Iris Dailey for this quote which is now embedded into my everyday life: 'Feed your brain good stuff'! What I mean by this is instead of mindlessly scrolling through social media to fill your time there are plenty of alternatives that can help you step into the happiest version of yourself.

Books

Why not start reading a book about a subject you are passionate about? Well, clearly you are already doing that if you are reading this right now. But what I mean is, why stop here? There is so much to learn and you never know what book you could stumble upon that may just change your whole outlook on life.

Podcasts

I love podcasts because it feels like you are just having a chat with a friend. I listen to many podcasts for many different reasons, to motivate me, to make me laugh and to educate myself. Here are some of my favourites . . .

◇ 'Highest Self Podcast' by Sahara Rose

◇ 'The Self Love Fix' by Beatrice Kamau

◇ 'The Dominating Edge' by Jeff Hammer

- ◇ 'The Diary Of A CEO' by Steven Bartlett

- ◇ 'That's So Sabotage' by Emma, Sophie and Nits

- ◇ 'Call Her Daddy' by Alex Cooper

Social Media

Don't get me wrong, I do love a good social media scroll and I do believe we can utilize social media to be beneficial to our mental health rather than destroying it. This is simply done by following people who uplift and inspire us rather than make us feel shit about ourselves. Even though that is not their fault, if you find yourself constantly comparing yourself to someone else, just unfollow them, then start the inner work and focus on your own happiness.

'Step into the
happiest version
of yourself.'

CRYSTALS FOR HAPPINESS

Sunstone

◇◇◇◇◇◇◇

Sunstone is the ultimate feel-good crystal and can help provide you with the extra dose of vitamin D needed to chase away those darker days. This stone will bring you a sense of optimism and an inner peace in knowing that everything will turn out well in the near future. It is an excellent stone to attract good fortune, prosperity and promotion. Sunstone will bring positivity into all areas of your life that are causing you unhappiness. The very nature of this crystal's energy is centred around feelings of joy and, as I said in chapter two, it is literal sunshine in a stone and a crystal I would recommend to absolutely everyone.

Labradorite

◇◇◇◇◇◇◇

If you feel like you are stuck in a rut and want to encourage fun in your life, this is the stone for you. Known as 'the stone of magic', the rainbow flashes within a Labradorite crystal hold the energy to bring the magic back into your life and attract new, exciting possibilities. This beautiful stone will renew your zest for life and inspire feelings of creativity, pushing you to become the happiest version of yourself. Labradorite is said to relieve feelings of insecurity, depression and anxiety, all whilst boosting confidence in your own abilities.

Lapis Lazuli

◇◇◇◇◇◇◇◇

This stunning deep-blue crystal flecked with white and gold is known for amplifying feelings of positivity and happiness. As well as this, it is great at encouraging open and honest communication. Although honesty isn't always easy, being able to truthfully communicate your needs and desires to others is imperative to your overall mental wellbeing. By bringing honesty and a sense of openness into all of your interactions, Lapis Lazuli will allow you to speak your truth and live authentically, which I personally believe is the key to real happiness.

Carnelian

◇◇◇◇◇◇◇◇

Carnelian is, above all, a crystal of personal happiness and fulfilment. Being the ultimate stone of confidence, it will allow you to demand what you truly desire out of life. Many people know what will make them happy but lack the confidence to really go for it, resulting in them settling for the easier or safer route. Carnelian will help remove these negative feelings of self-doubt and really push you to follow your dreams!

Sodalite

◇◇◇◇◇◇◇◇

If you are an overthinker, like myself, Sodalite is a must-have! Known as 'the stone of logic', this calming crystal emits a tranquil energy that clears the mind and provokes deep thought. This is a great crystal for those who tend to let their thoughts run away with them as it gives them the ability to see things from a more logical and rational perspective. Sodalite is also great at boosting feelings of self-esteem and self-trust, so no matter what life throws at you, you will have the confidence of knowing everything will be okay in the end!

YOU ARE THE MASTER OF YOUR OWN HAPPINESS

Looking after yourself and your energy is going to play a huge part in your overall happiness. If you take one thing away from this chapter, or even from this whole book, I hope it is the fact that the only person who holds the key to your happiness is you. Happiness is a choice you can make every day, in all the small things all around you, but in order to get to that point it's imperative to address any emotional wounds that need healing. Let me be clear, if you have trauma that you haven't healed from fully, you are CERTAINLY not broken, and no, you do not need to be fixed. But, my point is you owe it to yourself to live the happiest, most fulfilling life possible and sometimes you have to pull out some weeds so that the flowers can grow.

Another piece of advice is that it is not selfish to put your own happiness and needs first. Whilst writing this book my step-mum, even though we hate that term, gave me some advice. She said, 'On an aircraft in an emergency you are told to put your own oxygen mask on first before helping others.' Meaning you need to look after yourself first before you can help anyone else or be of use to anyone else. Also, people in general, but especially women, are made to feel guilty about putting themselves first or 'treating' themselves (this can be anything from buying yourself something new or getting your hair done to going to an exercise class), but we need to look after ourselves first in order to be able to look after others.

CONCLUSION

Well then, beautiful people, that brings us to the end of this book but also to the beginning of your journey. I hope you have enjoyed reading it even half as much as I have loved writing it! So allow me to leave you with some parting spiritual big sister advice before you embark on this exciting new journey . . .

Although crystals have been an absolute game-changer for me when it comes to creating the life of my dreams, I want to really emphasize that your true power is already WITHIN YOU. When you are asking for things from the universe it is important to remember you ARE the universe. The unlimited source of potential and power is within you. So, the most powerful tool you can use to assist you along your journey going forward is your mindset. If you can master the art of positive thinking, you can master anything. Crystals will simply work alongside you to amplify your energy, but just know that if you desire anything, you can have it.

If, after reading this book, you are still struggling with the process of manifestation, it may just be the case that you need to look at it from a different perspective. Obviously, mindset is crucial, and putting positive thoughts and intentions out to the universe is the main goal. You may have heard previously about manifesting and crystals, and more specifically this narrative that you can simply ask the universe for what you want and then just sit back and let it happen. Well, that will work but it will take a hell of a long time. Think of it this way, your manifestation, or goal, is your destination. It's where you want to be, it's where you are trying to get to. The only person who is going to get you there is you. Your manifestation represents the energy you use to reach your destination. You could put the energy into walking to your destination – it would take a lot longer, but you don't have to use up too much energy doing so. However, you could take this manifestation energy and use it as you would use petrol to fill up a car. So you have a car, it's full up with petrol, but guess what? You are not going anywhere unless you step on the gas. In this very long-winded metaphor I am using, the 'gas' is inspired action. You can ask the universe for what you desire and it will line up the easiest route for you to travel to your destination; the universe will act as your GPS or navigation system. But unless YOU put your foot down on that pedal and start taking action towards that goal, it is going to take you a very long time to get there. For example, if you are trying to manifest a bigger booty (someone actually asked me this the other day which is why it's popped into my mind), you can sit there with all the positive intention of growing your booty but unless you get that booty in a gym, you're going to be waiting a little while.

The universe does this amazing thing when you manifest; acting as your GPS it will put everything into place for you. Like with that booty example, you may start hearing a lot about certain gyms or exercises more, or get introduced to people who can share their own personal tips that can help you grow your booty, but the true key to unlocking your manifestation lies with you! Going back to the car metaphor, when you implement crystals into your life, you can think of this as adding a rocket launcher to the back of this hypothetical car. Crystals work so well at amplifying the energy of what you are trying to manifest, when you learn to work with them alongside taking inspired action towards your goals – you will be unstoppable.

ACKNOWLEDGEMENTS

There are lots of people I need to thank for assisting me along my journey of writing this book, so buckle in. First and foremost, Fenella Bates, the wonderful publisher at Penguin who approached me about writing this book and has wholeheartedly believed in me and encouraged me every step of the way. Also, Paula Flanagan, an editor at Penguin, and the whole Penguin team for their support and for providing me with lots of flowers and booze along the way!

Next up, a massive thank you to my two younger sisters, Tabby and Eliza, also known as my 'minions', due to them practically running my whole business so that I could write this book – I couldn't have done it without you. That leads me on to the other members of my family. Dad, thank you for always encouraging me to do whatever I want in life and for inspiring me every day. Step-mum Emma, thank you for always being top cheerleader and also for not telling everyone on your Facebook about this book before you were allowed to – I know you were so proud you nearly burst. Thank you to my mum Lisa for letting me come over every week for cuddles with my newest little sister, Olivia-Grace – those little visits gave me the motivation to keep pushing through and to make you both proud. I would also like to thank all my crazy aunties, uncles and cousins for everything they have done for me growing up; we are not only family, we are friends, and you have all played such a huge part in the person I am today. Finally, in terms of family, thank you to my grandparents.

To the Easterbrook grandparents for being such an inspiration to me growing up, I could write a whole new book on how much you have done for me, thank you. To the Treacy grandparents who encouraged me to apply for a poetry competition run by Travelodge in 2010 after seeing my passion for writing. Thank you for taking me to the opening of the hotel where I could see my first-place winning poem proudly displayed on the walls of Travelodge's reception, labelled as 'Horsham's Sleeping Poet'. Thank you to the Farrell grandparents, particularly my Nanny Farrell for passing down her witchy ways to me.

Now that's family done, I want to give a special shout-out to my friends . . . my housemate Dharma, thank you for always being on hand with a glass of savvy b when needed and for always listening to hours of me ranting. Soph, thank you for showing me that with hard work, a girl can really achieve anything – you are incredible. A special thank you to Sasha, Beth and Emma for being designated therapists and for reminding me to have fun when life can get overwhelming. Kitty, Bam, Zola, Georgia and Morgan, or more commonly known as 'gin in a tin', you ladies all inspire me so much every day. To be surrounded by such a fiercely independent, loyal, supportive group of girls has been such a blessing, not just during the writing of this book but throughout my whole life. I am eternally grateful for you.

281

INDEX

283

285

◆ INDEX

287

PENGUIN MICHAEL JOSEPH

UK | USA | Canada | Ireland | Australia
India | New Zealand | South Africa

Penguin Michael Joseph is part of the Penguin Random House group of companies
whose addresses can be found at global.penguinrandomhouse.com

Penguin
Random House
UK

First published 2023
001

Images on pp. 24, 27, 68, 187 © Content Pixie/Unsplash; p. 79 © Igumnova Irina/Shutterstock.com; p. 83 ©
Ingemar Magnusson/Alamy Stock Photo; p. 105 © Karolina Grabowska/Unsplash; p. 109 © Cami Cam/
Unsplash; p. 113 © Hanasaki/Shutterstock.com; p. 113 © Hanasaki/Shutterstock.com; p.121 © Capitolio
Arts/Shutterstock.com; p. 134–135 © Esther Verdú/Unsplash; p. 181 © AveryKlein/Unsplash; p. 198 © Jirik
V/Shutterstock.com; p. 237 © MikaM/Shutterstock.com; p. 267 © Chandra Oh/Unsplash. Journal pages ©
AliceCam/Shutterstock.com and My Stock Photos/Shutterstock.com. All remaining images: © Moa
Thörneby. With thanks to the author, Charlie's Rock Shop and Amy Clarke for the loan of crystals
for this book.

Set in Voyage, Runalto, Juana, Brandon Grotesque

Typeset by Maeve Bargman
Colour reproduction by Altaimage, London
Printed and bound in Italy by L.E.G.O. SpA

The authorized representative in the EEA is Penguin Random House Ireland,
Morrison Chambers, 32 Nassau Street, Dublin D02 YH68

A CIP catalogue record for this book is available from the British Library

ISBN: 978–0–241–62659–7

www.greenpenguin.co.uk

MIX
Paper from
responsible sources
FSC® C018179

Penguin Random House is committed to a
sustainable future for our business, our readers
and our planet. This book is made from Forest
Stewardship Council® certified paper.